Profound Writings from Everyday People

by
Cynthia Attar

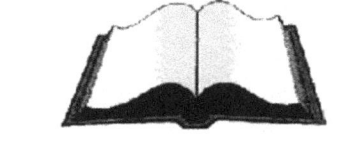

CCB Publishing
British Columbia, Canada

Profound Writings from Everyday People

Copyright © 2012 by Cynthia Attar
ISBN-13: 978-1-927360-68-2
Fifth Edition

Library and Archives Canada Cataloguing in Publication
Attar, Cynthia
Profound Writings from Everyday People / by Cynthia Attar – 5th ed.
Previous title: Profound words from common people.
Includes bibliographical references and index
ISBN 978-1-927360-68-2
1. Spiritual journals--Authorship. 2. Spiritual life.
3. Self-actualization (Psychology). I. Title.
BL624.A87 2012   204'.4   C2012-903734-6

Cover design by Raquel Cuellar: www.raquelcuellar.com

Extreme care has been taken to ensure that all information presented in this book is accurate and up to date at the time of publishing. Neither the author nor the publisher can be held responsible for any errors or omissions. Additionally, neither is any liability assumed for damages resulting from the use of the information contained herein.

All rights reserved. No part of this publication may be reproduced, stored in a retrieval system, or transmitted in any form or by any means, electronic, mechanical, photocopying, recording or otherwise without the express written permission of the author. Printed in the United States of America, the United Kingdom, and Australia.

Address all inquiries to:
Cynthia Attar
28500 Hwy 24
Sunnyside, WA 98944

Publisher: CCB Publishing
              British Columbia, Canada
              www.ccbpublishing.com

A Note of Appreciation

Thank you to all contributors and their profound submissions-which made this book possible.

Thank you to Raquel Cuellar
for the design and artwork on the book's cover.

CONTENTS

Chapter 1:   Introducing Profound Writings 1
Chapter 2:   "How To" and Pitfalls 10
   How To 10
      The difference between ego-self and god-self 12
   Pitfalls 13
      Unbalanced desire 13
      Limiting beliefs 14
      Fear 15
      Inadequate inner peace 16
      Trying too hard 17
Chapter 3:   Transitioning from Ego-Self to God-Self Writings 21
   The Transition 21
Chapter 4:   Who Can Have These Chats? 39
Chapter 5:   Who Are You, Upstairs? 49
Chapter 6:   Why Aren't Some Hearing You? 56
Chapter 7:   The Purpose of Life 67
Chapter 8:   When to Help and When to Allow? 82
Chapter 9:   Where Does Money Fit into Our Lives? 94
Chapter 10: What's Up With Fear? 103
Chapter 11: Please Clarify Feelings 113
Chapter 12: Today's Youth 128
Chapter 13: The Significance of Family 142
Chapter 14: Serving the World and Creating Our Life 147
   Serving the World 147
   Self-Creating Our Lives 150
Chapter 15: Oneness—Asked by Tiaka/Japan 153
Chapter 16: Why Do We Fear Death? 160
Chapter 17: Animals, Nature, and the Earth 166
   Animals and Nature 166
   Humans: The Earth's Steward 169
EPILOGUE 174
INDEX OF PARTICIPANTS 175

Chapter 1
Introducing Profound Writings

Are you aware that you—yes, the person reading this right now—can bring forth amazing writings so profound that it will astonish you? Do you know that you naturally have the ability to tap into the universal library of knowledge and find perfect solutions to your problems? The truth is that everyone in the world is born with this ability, and it is available right inside of you.

Do you fervently desire to know your purpose in life? Do you somberly question why there is war, poverty, and suffering in the world? Do you have a longing to know what will happen when you die? Or do you simply question why your children are misbehaving? Would life change if you had answers to all these questions? What if you could be your own spiritual guru in a very short time?

Welcome to the glorious world of discovering and utilizing your god-self through free flow writing. Your god-self is a merging of the normal you—that part that is ego driven—with upstairs, that higher essence, that which some consider as god, to allow profound words to form on paper or computer screen. Other than free flow writing, expressing the god-self is accomplished in many forms and ways.

Have you ever watched a ballet dancer who seems to float effortlessly and magically on stage in an awe-inspiring performance? Have you ever admired the high level artist who puts simple colors and hues together to form an exquisite masterpiece of a painting? Have you ever become lost in an author's words on pages which have filled all your senses in an absorbing drama too intense to put down? These are examples of when people have opened up to allow upstairs to work through them as their god-self. In the same manner, a writer can ask a life altering question, get out of the way, and allow their god-self to answer that question through free flow, automatic writing that leads to profound messages on paper.

This book introduces the idea that tapping into higher intelligence by way of free flow writing can be available by anyone; and to provide "how-to" in discovering the key to unlock that inner resource door. These pages also provide plenty of examples of profound god-self writings from people just like you— everyday folks living all around the globe—whom have learned to tap into this profound source.

This task of funneling down knowledge from higher up does not require a stint of residing on a mountaintop for months or years. You don't need to be a "chosen one" or learn to channel non-physical entities to access this high information. Words and messages, logical yet profound, can actually be yours for the taking, if you so desire. You just have to resonate with it, allow it, practice it, and you will soon be writing amazing, profound messages from universal intelligence. With each of us having the innate ability to reveal answers to life's difficult questions, we only need to discover the keys that unlock this precious gift of connection to the universal source, to upstairs.

Why is free flow writing a better way to connect than other ways? The writing aspect of allowing upstairs to come through you is quite direct. As opposed to an abstract painting that doesn't need to make logical sense when completed, in free flow writing you must take the pictures, ideas, feelings that enter your mind and then translate them to written, completed thoughts. It forces you to slow down the energy running through, to dig deeper, which pushes you to become more clear on the message at hand. With free flow writing, you are left with more than a spiritually memorable performance or a highly inspired masterpiece, you are left with actual words, direct messages, and personal insights. With free flow writing you can get tangible answers in response to your most asked questions. Besides, some of us are not natural artists or dancers, but most of us can put thoughts down onto paper in the form of sentences!

For this book to illustrate the depth of conversation that is possible when one accesses their god-self through writing, I set out to find people already doing this work. It only took an internet connection and a few emails to find exactly what I was seeking. I found a pocket of people who were thrilled with the possibility of getting their secret inner writings out to the public. Most were excited to be an integral part of assisting those ready for this teaching. Who were these folks? Were they accomplished writers? Were they of a certain religious organization, or high up on the path of enlightenment? Were they gifted or more intelligent than the ordinary person?

The folks who submitted writings for this book came from all walks of life, from various countries, from a menagerie of religious and spiritual-based backgrounds. These people are as common as you and I. The main difference is that they know it is possible, and they know they are capable of tapping into upstairs. You will soon see how profoundly wise these everyday people are! Once I gathered these folks together, each week I submitted the same question to each of them. They took precious time out of busy schedules to tap into their god-self and write the answer to my directed question. I was thrilled, amazed, sometimes even overwhelmed in receiving very high level answers to my questions. With this, I began to form the book you are reading now.

"Give a man a fish and you feed him for a day.
Teach a man to fish and you feed him for a lifetime."

The first chapters are devoted to the "how-to" work. The following chapters are the meat, the really juicy wisdom. These chapters consist of one question with a variety of god-self answers to that question.

The participants were not privy to anyone else's answers until all answers were submitted. As you will see, the variety of answers have a strong common thread, regardless of the fact that each participant had vastly different upbringings when it came to their personal, religious, or spiritual beliefs.

The answers below were selected for submission as they posed the clearest connection and communication from upstairs. The participants agreed to be anonymous, (names have been changed) to allow freedom of word flow in case the subject matter became personally revealing. They have addressed me using my internet name of "Llovit". The chats presented in this book are *exactly as received by the submitter*, even without perfect sentence structure or grammar. To keep the messages pure, the only thing I changed was a bit of spelling and punctuation for clarity. Periodically, you will find words or phrases enclosed in brackets [ ]. In the brackets I have inserted additional information to add to clarity. If words or phrases are enclosed in parenthesis ( ), it is the author or upstairs presenting a side note.

To make the words to follow clear, I have assigned specific styles to specific words. These will become apparent very soon.

Narration: Times New Roman-normal

Participant: Times New Roman bold italic

Questions: Indented, Times New Roman italic

God-self: Arial normal

Llovit in dialogue (not narration): Indented Arial bold font

Below is an example of an introductory conversation I had with upstairs. Even though I like to use the word "upstairs", the participants seem to like to use other words, such as source, universal intelligence, God, or god. Whatever name they have put to their writings was fine with me. The following is a taste of what you will be able to do once that door is opened, and what many people have presented later in this book.

Upstairs, what message would you like to share with the readers right now?

Hello to all and welcome. It is possible, likely, simple, and necessary for the accelerated evolvement of the soul—due to earth changes—to receive guidance from your inner god-self. What is the inner god-self? Well, imagine a huge library with every book answering exactly what you are questioning. Deep inside you have your own personal Internet—without the ads!—a grand source of universal knowledge, higher perspective of your problems, and decision making capabilities. Not to mention the means to inner peace, joy, love, and connection. And it's all TRUTH. You want to know truths...well tapping in will connect you with YOUR TRUTH—which is the only truth there actually is.

What is the purpose of this book?

This book is a preliminary source of information for those who have an attraction to tap into the ultimate source of wisdom, knowledge, and life workings. It is not a book for everyone and I caution anyone to not push this book on those who do not pose an interest in this work. It is you, the reader, whom we have presented this book to; and it is you, the reader, who is in the position of utilizing this book to its full potential.

This book will aid you to tap into god within. Why is that an important thing to do? Well, for one, it is the way of the future. Soon, intellect alone will be much outdated, primitive. When one combines the human intellect with their inner god-self, then and only then, will the fullness and richness of life, of this earthly project, the ultimate outcome, be of service to self and others. Let me explain this a bit more clearly.

When one taps only into human intellect, they tap into a surface layer of knowledge. Think of logic as the cream in a gallon jar of fresh milk just taken from the cow. The cream has arisen to the top, yet the rest of the milk is the bulk of your being, the god part of the self. Many people are only aware of the cream (ego/conscious) and do not ever venture past that top layer. When one learns to find the milk (the god-self), one then has access to the most valuable part of that glass jar.

The intellect has its purpose and is extremely vital to the human mind, to the human life, to the progression of the soul. Do not discount the value of the intellect, as without it humans would be not much different than animals—your dog or cat for instance. Dogs and cats do not possess the human intellect. Now, that is not saying they cannot reason, cannot have feelings, cannot comprehend, as they can. The difference is that humans have a desire to push forth, to overcome, to create, and to appreciate in a way that pets do not chose to do at this time. Therefore, when one views a dog, one sees the instinctual and the intuitive (or the milk). One sees the soul in action. Yet, dogs are not ones that strive for perfection, strive for this or that. Dogs just are. Dogs are the example of what humans want to achieve in the soul area. Yet some mistake the soul as being the only important part of the human makeup.

Yes, the intellect has gotten the human into big trouble. And it also has gotten the human into fabulous developments and progression. However, the solution is to incorporate the soul seen in the dog, with the intellect seen in the human, all in one body. This, my friends, is the next stage of humans, the bridging of the gap between the soul and the intellect. This has not yet been achieved on this planet worldwide in this lifetime, but soon most will be there.

It is in this bridging that we bring you this book as a preliminary step to this transformation of humans. You may dismiss this as rubbish, or you may feel the truth in your soul of this information. Whichever you choose is perfectly right for you at this time. We honor all of you in whatever phase of humanity you choose to reside. If you choose to forge ahead with this project of tapping into your own inner god, then it is to your benefit, as to the benefit of every other person on this planet. If it feels right to continue this process, by all means, let's continue—you and I—as we embark on this exciting journey together.

Okay, I understand that accessing my god-self is a good thing. Why would I learn this skill, other than to prepare for the future? What's in it for me today?

When one is in the formidable stage, one asks such questions. This is excellent, as it states that you are interested in furthering this pursuit, desiring to move in this direction. My answer to you is a question; Do you long to further your evolution? Do you want to progress on a spiritual path quickly? Do you desire to gain added wisdom and knowledge? If these answers are yes, this process will give you the means, the reason, the incentive to do all of these things mentioned above.

If the answer is no, then there is another path that is in your best interests. And we further recommend searching for just the right words, methods, feelings, posed in other publications. It is perfectly natural and perfectly okay to do so. We do not mind, as we know that "all paths lead to Rome", and you will eventually get to a god-self connection in your own manner. You see, that is the Rome that all paths lead to. All paths lead to God. All paths lead to connecting with your god-self, which leads to the upcoming human transformation.

Can one transform without tapping into their god-self?

Of course they can. However, the transition may not be as pleasant or smooth, or as much fun. Without connecting within, one is left to guess at what is happening to them. This breeds fear, confusion, misdiagnosis of the situation, etc. When the ability to tap in has been developed and is strong, one has all the answers needed at just the right and perfect time for a fuller experience, with less confusion and fear in the process.

So, what type of answers do you give us when we learn to tap into you? Like, are there some answers that you do not have or cannot relate to me? Say, I asked you a technical science question where I have no knowledge of the answer, but researchers DO have the answer. Will you tell me the answer?

This is not a play toy. This is not a way to bypass education and learning. This is not a game with which to monitor your ego. We ask that you question your questions and see where that answer gets you. What you NEED to know—what is necessary for your spiritual evolvement and growth of the soul—we can help you to find your own answers. What you think are vitally important questions, may not be necessary for the path you have decided upon. Now you, in your current non-technical, non-science occupation, deciding to ask a technical question, most likely the answer will come to you in the words of a book, or in a feeling, an urge to go to the bookstore, or picking up a magazine at the doctor's office.

The answers you seek will come to you, but not in the form you are expecting. We are not an 'Ask Jeeves organization [now it is Ask.com, an Internet company where you ask any off the wall question and instantly you have the answer], but we may be able to help direct you to the answer, if your thoughts are on the question consistently. Many thoughts come and go so quickly that those answered/acted upon are those that you hold in your mind. Just know that if you are having a problem, most likely the answer will come to you as if looking at it from another perspective. Now, we say answers; however we are just suggesting to you to look at things from a higher perspective. That is to say that we will direct you to the library if you want to know about squirrel habitat, rather than telling you in direct words how squirrels live. That information is not necessary for the evolution of your soul therefore may not come out when you tap inside yourself.

And how about communicating with you? How do we?

We will delve further into this question in a later chapter. Just for now, let me say that one must become aware and utilize all methods of our communications. Let me list off some of the ways we talk to you:

- Feelings in your stomach area
- Words from another that ring true which have an impact
- The imaginary sightings or hearings of something that creates you to change direction in thought or deed

The very message you seek may be in a book or magazine. Pay attention to those publications you feel drawn towards. When in doubt about which feelings are from me, discuss and come up with a plan where in you know that it is a "God-message". Such as, Llovit and I have an agreement that if she is to benefit by reading a book, it will be in the used book section of the bookstore and not more than a set amount of money—set on the day of shopping. There is noting any inner feelings. One will soon learn which is from the highest good. Until you are certain, experiment with your feelings. Try them out, play with them, and make feelings your friend, not your enemy or something to fear. It is the most accurate path of communications with us. You will benefit immensely in this process. Thank you.

Okay upstairs, what else do the readers need to know before we get started?

Just to hang on for a grand ride—the ride of your life! There is no secret to this. You [all people] and I communicate all the time on other than a conscious level. We are simply bringing normal happenings to conscious realization. Fear not. Question your previous teachings if there is a belief in the way. Such as a belief in the devil, sin, etc., which creates a blockage to communicating with me/us. [More on this later.]

When one acknowledges such beliefs, it is a grand day for us, as the doors swing wider for our thoughts to enter to you and you to accept them; and we know that soon this difficulty will have a resolve for both of us. Thank you for reading this book. You will find yourself in many of the answers here. Hang on, the ride is just getting underway!

You are capable of writing such grand wisdom if you want to, as desire is the first key. The second key is a little bit of instruction (this book will provide you with an in-depth how-to). The third key is to practice. Soon, you will be astonished at what insight and wisdom comes out on the paper or computer in front of you—not unlike the wisdom writings found in later chapters.

I would like to personally thank you for picking up this book and having the courage to move upwards and onwards for yourself and therefore for those around you.

Chapter 2
"How To" and Pitfalls

Before we get into the delicious part of presenting the profound free flowing answers to directed questions, it is our desire to first assist you in developing your own means to connect with upstairs. This chapter and the next consist of philosophy and the how-to portion of this book, as well as troubleshooting if words are not flowing freely.

In a nutshell, the main reason to do this work is to learn to connect to the higher part of yourself, to universal intelligence, and be able to attain a clear, written, two way communication level between self and upstairs, your god-self. This will give you access to very high wisdom for all requested answers.

This chapter we will clarify and differentiate between the god-self and the ego-self—that part of you that you *think* is you. And to help you to locate that place inside where you can find your soul essence. We also will explore some common obstacles and pitfalls that people have in attempting this work. After this how-to chapter, the next chapter will show chats which obtained that crossover state transitioning from ego-self to god-self through free flow writings. This chapter is very educational as well as revealing.

How To

One method to practice finding that link to upstairs within and to help you along this process is continuous writing in a free flow manner. To do this, find a physical spot at home, or even in the library, out in nature, or anywhere where distractions are at a minimum. This may require you to mute the TV, turn off the stereo, or lock yourself in the bedroom, or tell your spouse to watch the kids for an hour. Get relaxed with pen and notebook in hand or sitting comfortably at a computer. Now, just pick a subject of interest and start writing (translate these instructions if typing on a computer). Just write non-stop in a totally free flow style. Write at least three continuous pages in a row, starting with that subject as a jumping off point, but allowing other subjects to filter in or take over if they so choose. Write with no breaks or hesitations. Don't worry if the words make little sense, or the sentences don't fit together. Just write non-stop. If you don't know what to write, write "I don't know what to write". Just keep the pen flowing uninterrupted on the paper. When finished with your three pages of gibberish, set it aside until tomorrow.

Do this free flow writing practice daily. It helps if you pick a subject of current interest to write about and just start writing. Soon you will become aware of that white space, that slightly ajar door between thoughts. That is where the bleed-through will happen. Within a few sessions you will find messages or thoughts from upstairs in amongst those seemingly unconnected words and phrases. Don't try and write words from upstairs, just allow whatever comes through.

As you practice your daily free flow writing, just write down any feelings that have arisen. Write to explain the pictures in your mind. There is a short transition period of fluently translating those thoughts, pictures, feelings into actual words on paper. Just do your best, and know that it will become easier with practice. When we were children, we had thoughts we could not express in words. We had to learn language to be heard. This is similar, in that we again have images and thoughts we must translate, but this time we translate into the written word.

How will you know what you are getting is from something higher? It may start with a simple word or phrase that feels subtly different than your own—sort of like the phrase came from somewhere else, but it still could have come from your own thoughts. Continue on this project until you find more and more of these gray area phrases that may not be from you, and consider the possibility that it is upstairs talking. Keep writing the three non-stop pages until you can feel the difference between that which is you and that which has a slightly different/higher feel. Don't over analyze, just pay a bit of attention to increase your awareness.

Here is a test if you are unsure is what is coming out is from the highest good or from your ego mind. Take one of my questions posed later in this book. Write down the question on a note pad or key it into your computer. Pretend you are going to send your answer to me for possible submission. Now, get quiet and begin writing your answer. If you notice yourself writing, rewriting, editing, changing the words around until you get it just right, then you probably have not tapped into upstairs, but into your ego-self. However, if what you have just written needs no editing, no changing, it is positive and has no negativity within it, if it feels good and sounds true to you, if it is perfectly understood and clear, then most likely you have found upstairs inside and are accessing this special part of yourself. Congratulations, you hit the mark! Another clue is when the response from your writing surprises you or makes you laugh as though someone said something you weren't prepared for.

Once you get efficient at finding god-self words, these words are easily accessible anywhere. Personally, I now do some really good upstairs chatting at the local coffee counter of a truck stop restaurant with the bustle of hungry customers, and the wait staff buzzing around like bees. My favorite style of chatting is with pen and paper. I buy spiral notebooks in bulk and keep one in my car, one in my traveling bag, and several at home. At one time when money was extremely tight, I had several chats on the back of paper placemats at diners!

The difference between ego-self and god-self

Sometimes people get caught up in not knowing what is ego-self writings and what is god-self writings. Here's an analogy of the difference between ego-self and god-self. The logical, rational, opinion part of you (also known as ego) resides in one part of the mind. This is where you house your fears, beliefs, limitations, judgments, opinions and is occupied with work, home, money, power, family and the desire to prove you are right. It is the you that you think is you. This is what we refer to as the ego-self.

The other part of you, the god part, holds the direct upstairs connection. Here is where we are able to tap into the universal source and come up with wisdom not readily available in the ego state. In everyday life, we primarily are consciously using the ego part of the mind. The upstairs part is that which we are learning to tap into—on a conscious level—with these free flow writings.

Now, that doesn't mean the ego is a bad thing. It is in the ego which lie filters that somewhat askew the message coming through from upstairs. This is actually an asset. This means that your filtered words, writing, music, painting, dancing or whatever creative endeavor you attend to will be slightly different than another's. The human, channeling upstairs, merges the two in an exquisite flow. It is what makes your upstairs chats *your* truth, *your* reality, *your* soul's evolution, *your god-self*.

Is accessing your god-self easy? Well, it might come easily to you or it might not. Once you believe it's possible, obtain the humble desire to do this work, clear the pathway, access the necessary mental state, and practice fluently, then it is an easy task. For some folks, all the above falls together fairly quickly and the process is easy. For others, the desire to tap into upstairs could be peppered with obstacles—which may require clearing before this act is accomplished with a pure flow. It just may be possible that these obstacles have come to the surface for a resolve, not only for this work, but for other areas of your life. The pitfalls that seem to come up most are unbalanced desire, limiting beliefs, fear, lack of adequate inner peace, lack of practice, and trying too hard. Let me delve into these possible difficulties.

Pitfalls

Unbalanced desire

Examine your desire to do this work. What is the real reason you want to access that wisdom within? This is a very good question to ask, and to answer truthfully. The answer could be the pivoting point on if you will successfully access that link to upstairs within. In my quest to find participants for this project, invariably there would be a few who would send an email offering to answer all my questions. "Just ask me anything. I can answer any question," the person would claim. Through experience I learned to be leery of these offers.

So, what's wrong with that offer? S/he is just trying to help someone (me) who seems to be looking for that perfect person who has all the answers, right? Look again. Where is the person most likely coming from? If this person claims to have all answers for all questions, then that person can not possibly come up with information that is unknown to him/her. In his/her mind and belief, s/he has life all figured out. When the focus is on ego gratification, it detracts, hinders, or even prevents the humble state of mind needed to go within and find something grander than one's ego-self.

Accessing upstairs happens when I sit down with my spiral notebook, write a question, and soften the focus of my mind. With no expectations I allow the pen to move freely. Those truly tapping into upstairs within don't have all the answers, but we know where to find most of them! In that slight twist of consciousness, lo and behold, soon we begin receiving thoughts, pictures, feelings—turned into words—which seem to show up from out of nowhere! That is the beauty of discovering the god-self. So, in summary, the desire to do this work is grand. But the balanced reason for the desire is the key that unlocks that door to your god-self.

Limiting beliefs

Your beliefs can also dictate if you do this work or not. If you have had certain religious upbringings, you may have learned that it was impossible for god to speak with you personally. To have the nerve to think that god would speak to you right there inside of your mind would be blasphemy. How dare you suggest that self and god are one of the same? But maybe now you have moved away from that path, and are questioning if that whole train of thought is really your truth. Do you think you would be fluent in free flow writing if you believed you are not worthy of god talking to you? (This is one reason I prefer to state that which is higher than self as "upstairs" rather than "God", as it has less emotional inner discomfort for some people.)

Let's examine beliefs for a moment. A belief is only what you think is true. A belief is not absolute, not necessarily truth for everyone. A belief is actually a thought that you just keep thinking over and over. A belief limits a person's ability to see past that belief. Most beliefs cry and demand to be proven right. Such as, if I believe in only a particular type of god with certain qualities, ideas, desires, and requirements, then I am limiting myself to not explore other possibilities of what or who God could be.

Beliefs get changed all the time. How many beliefs have you changed since being a child? Thousands have been changed—hopefully! How about the belief that you couldn't ride a bike? Then one day Dad plopped you on that bike seat and stayed with you until you found that two-wheeled balance point. You came out of that experience with a changed belief, *"I can ride a bike!"* This book is plopping you on the seat, telling you that you can ride, showing other people like yourself who are riding around you, and trying to help you find that balance point for yourself. When you actually move forward with that front tire wiggling, just keep pedaling and balancing as best you can. You will make it! That old saying is absolutely true, "What you can conceive and believe, you can achieve."

Fear

Fear is an interesting state. What fear would arise if you actually could hear God speaking to you? Your thoughts may go something like this:

> **If I could hear God speaking just to me, what might she say? Geez, she probably would say I wasn't good enough. Look at all the mistakes I've made in my life. God would probably tell me I'm not right in my behaviors. I know that. I know I have hurt people. 'I really didn't mean to God--honest'. If I dared to start chatting with God, I know she would see through the facade I show the world. Oh man, if I really had to own up, I'd probably find I have been wrong for a big portion of my life. I don't want to have been wrong all this time, I just want to live as I have lived for all my life—good**

or bad. Well, no I don't. If I did, I wouldn't be at this point of trying to improve my life, I guess. Sheesh. Alright, if I did have a chat with God, and she showed me how wrong I have been, I may have to change how I relate to others. And if I did that, surely they would reject me. We got this secret pact, ya know. I say things, they get mad, and then they give me their power. I like it that way! But ...I really don't like it that way. If I changed that pattern, they may reject me. If they reject me, I may be totally alone. And if I am totally alone, well, then ...I ...may ...die.

Phew, finally got down to the core issue here. So, look at this linear thread. A simple inability to hear upstairs within could actually be rooted in ...well, a core fear of ...death. Yep, that would stop most folks! Interesting how fears work. So, the very best we can do is realize our true fears by freely allowing whatever words to show up, such as above, until the core fear reveals itself and there is no more to say or write. Once we have the real issue at hand, there are a number of ways to resolve it. The hardest part is to identify the problem that is in the way.

Inadequate inner peace

The next most common pitfall is inadequate inner peace or quieting of the mind. As I don't have to tell you, when your mind is constantly occupied with chatter, it would be next to impossible to gather the frame of mind necessary for this work. When the TV is blasting, the kids are whining, the boss is demanding, and your spouse expects, you may not have it inside you to find your god within. And maybe that is why you have chosen your life as hectic as it is, for a really good excuse to not do this work! Getting to a place of inner peace and quieting of the mind is truly essential.

It is not a requirement to be a Zen meditation expert to find your inner peace. However for many reasons, meditation is a really good practice to bring into your daily routine. For one, it allows you to silence the mind of its normal chatter. And two, it keeps stress at bay. If a sitting meditation is not quite to your liking, take a walk in the woods, go jogging with the dog, settle into a comfy recliner and listen to the quiet in a still house. Along the same lines, clutter in ones living space aids to clutter in the mind. The cleaner and more organized your home, workplace, and yard, the easier it is to achieve inner peace.

I have this spot on my porch I like to sit and stare out into the woods with a blank mind. For some time, there were obstacles in the path of my favorite view. Here sat an old range needing to be taken to the dump, wire for the fence to be constructed and a big pile of branches pruned from the surrounding trees. All these things create a measure of disarray—virtually undetectable to the conscious mind—and are roadblocks to inner peace. Being sensitive to energies, I could actually feel the clutter in my mind when I sat at my favorite spot to try and absorb the peace of the woods. Once I removed these obstacles, I was able to clear my mind and again be in peace at those times.

One thing I would like to mention is that when I am heavily into some personal problem and I insist or demand answers, I may not get much response from upstairs. When one has an intense desire for a specific outcome, it may block the flow of those higher words. So, if I am attached to what I want the answer to be, I may get no true answer. This is extremely frustrating, but I have learned to just deal with knowing that I won't be able to tap in for answers during those really stressful times. Sometimes upstairs wants to talk about other things not quite so important.

Trying too hard

It is easy to expect something different than what you will get. Since our beliefs about God is that He's all powerful, all loving, and a part of everything; one may conclude that tapping into this tremendous source is like turning the hair dryer on and pointing it directly at your face. The expectation is that God's words are an unmistakable powerful blast. Some folks get frustrated when all obstacles seem to be out of the way, yet they cannot feel that immense power blasting at them. They conclude that they just cannot hear God, cannot even get close to hearing God, that they never will, and then finally they just quit trying.

Yes, the voice, words, feelings, energy, from upstairs is from an absolutely all-powerful source. However, it is the subtleties of the message that makes many people not recognize it and think it's just they talking. Expecting a power blast, one may not hear the whisper in the breeze. It is in this whisper that you will hear the voice of upstairs, simply and indiscriminately. With experience, you will become proficient at differentiating between the whisper of god and your own logical/opinion mind. Does this mean god is not logical? Not at all. Just note that god is all logical, but that doesn't mean that all logic is god.

A couple of our submitters addressed common blocks and helpful hints to connecting fully with upstairs.

Jay/Lismore/NSW/Australia

What's the best way of letting go of thoughts, feelings, and emotions?

Letting go of thoughts, feelings, and emotions is simply listening, accepting, acknowledging each; becoming an observer, not a participator. Each individual has free will to choose to do this in their own way, it is a gift. Some may see doing this as meditation; others may do this through being creative, etc. The principle is the same, surrendering to the moment, focus on the now breath and not attaching.

Patricia/NJ

Anytime fear, anger, negative emotions run rampant in a body/mind, there is:

Not enough [god] energy

Not enough clarity

The filters are stronger

Not enough time away from those emotions to allow a wild abundance of our energy to flow through.

The person may try and try to hear us, but other mish mash is in the way or is in the filter. If tapping into us is difficult for one who desires, step back a few steps and first learn to quiet the mind. That is the beginning of controlling your mind—to be able to control or stop the rampant raging, if only for a few moments.

There are many publications out there to guide you. Meditation, getting quiet, fantasizing, visualizing in a focused way, listening to the wind rustle through the trees, all are ways to begin to control the rampages of the mind and all its thoughts, feelings, emotions and such. Once much of the mish mash is swept aside for a few moments, our voice can then be heard by the recipient. The more balanced in nutrition, the easier a person can hear. Now, nutrition consists of any food or beverage that alters the chemical balance of the body, therefore the mind, too. Things to work on if tapping in isn't forthright:

- Study your body's food/liquid intake to create body/mind balance.
- Practice quieting the mind—first for a moment, and then daily until you can quiet the mind at will for however long you like.
- Trust that you can hear your inner god and that s/he is there and desires this communication also.
- Expect the subtle words to be god words. Don't expect god to speak loudly, forcefully. This work is an exercise on subtleties.

Encourage your readers to just write, type, talk as though they were talking to god and pretend like s/he is talking back. What would He say? Playing around with this is not only fun, but productive too.

In summary, if the humble desire to develop the god-self is intact, sit down to write your three non-stop pages every day. After a few sessions, if you just are not accomplishing this goal, examine your beliefs. See if fear is in the way. Note if you are able to quiet your mind at will. Don't try too hard. And listen for the subtle whispers and surprises of upstairs. Build on that daily, continuing the exercise of free-flow writing, until it becomes crystal clear of the difference between your opinion/ego words and your god-self words. Keep it up. Soon you will be successfully tapping into upstairs within and developing your god-self.

Chapter 3
Transitioning from Ego-Self to God-Self Writings

It is my wish that everyone have the tools ready at hand when they begin this work—which is now for many of you. For the transition chapter, I sought out people from outside the usual participant pool. Those who had just begun to tap into their god-self through free flow writing are presented below. It will help you identify the subtleness of the transition between normal everyday writing and free flowing god-self writings.

The Transition

It's warming to find those who have just discovered their god-self, and who want to share their excitement. Two of the participants, Lennie and Babysteps, began this book project by accessing their logical side for answers. With a little prodding, both show their magnificent transition in being able to find that link to upstairs within. Lennie sent me this opinion answer to the question: "Upstairs, if anyone can communicate with you, why are some people better than others at this?"

Lennie/OH/USA

To become an unlimited being, one must push through that barrier and find a way to access the god within. I have created a "possibility" of who I am. It calls me forth to be a better person—minute by minute—every day of my life. Who I am is the possibility of love fully expressed and that is who I am.

So when "life" happens I can stop and say that sentence in my head and choose whether I want to "be love" or not. I wish I could say that it is automatic for me to choose "love" but it is not. When I am present to the possibility—it is easier to choose....

There are times when I am in breakdown with all of this and I have enrolled lots of people into being coaches for me. I tell people who I am as possibility and ask them to HOLD ME ACCOUNTABLE to it!!! Some people understand—some don't. Spiritually, I have 4 coaches—two really close ones. They believe in me when I can't believe in myself.

These are heartfelt words to ponder, but the source of this writing is coming from Lennie's ego-self. As with a few others, I sent Lennie an email where I asked them to dig deeper, for that higher connection. Below is her response to my probing.

Lennie/OH/USA

You [Llovit] had sent me the note on "...you have answered through your logic..." It didn't make sense to me. Now, I get it!! WOW! This is going to be TOTALLY different for me. My initial response is "I can't write like that." And God is telling me

Yes, you can!!! That's why you're here—to learn how to know me on that level!!!

COOL!!! I must admit, I have a fear here with answering your [Llovit's] questions from the god within. Please be patient. I need some time to get clear on the fear so I can move past it. I think I'll need some coaching on this.

> **Llovit:** Hey, Lennie, instead of answering the question, how about writing down your fears/concerns? That would be most helpful to the readers. This 'discussion' can be to yourself, to me, to god, (even if s/he doesn't answer you) to whomever you want. Spill your guts, in other words. Maybe start with "I don't want to talk to god because..." I know I am asking for some tough stuff, Lennie. Looking forward to hearing from you!

Ok, Llovit, I'll take your suggestion on! I'm going to write a stream of consciousness. I have the house to myself and some beautiful music playing. I KNOW God is within me and God is ALWAYS encouraging me to 'be' more than I am.

I don't want to answer questions from the God within me because...
THAT WILL MEAN THAT I AM POWERFUL BEYOND MEASURE!!! And that scares me!!!

I resist. While I was typing, I realized that I was answering my own questions as God. Oh, this is what Llovit is looking for! And yet, when I go to answer your questions I am stopped. They must be too direct for me. They confront me—stop me. Sometimes I feel soooo lost in all of this. I woke up spiritually and I don't have a clear path to take. There is no control here. I have this sign up at my desk "Trust God, Trust the Journey" and yes, I know God will only provide LOVE. That IS really cool!!!! And yet it frightens me. It is TOO big for me.

No, it's not Lennie. I wouldn't put you here in this place this time if it wasn't perfect for you. You've gotten very good at listening but you resist. You resist a lot and that takes sooo much energy. When are you going to trust me and follow me completely?

I don't know.

If not now, when?

How? How do I do that? Trust you completely?

Oh Llovit, I lost it. I lost God. That was so weird. God was really answering me and I got scared. I'm just going to keep typing and see what happens. That was just too weird. Ok, so what was so weird about it? You know God talks to you—yeah—but this was soooo direct. So much, so very inside of me. A warm cozy feeling. It was wonderful, beautiful.

So why did you stop?

Phone rang—had to answer it. It might be my son Ben.

Had to answer it Lennie or did you just jump at the chance to get away from me?

Why would I ever want to get away from you?

Why indeed.

Help me God, help me make sense of all of this.

Do you really want to?

Yes.

Okay, then keep listening, keep doing all that you are doing. Stop resisting me. Listen, really listen.

There is that fear again.

Fear's okay. Please make fear your friend. Your life would go so much smoother. Trust in me completely. Let no one tell you that your path is not the correct one for there is no correct path. Each one is different and I am directing you, helping point out the way for you. You have declared to me that you want to make a huge difference in the world and you have no idea what that looks like.

Very good. I like the no attachment to the results.

You must listen. I'm sending you the signals, the path, the guidance that you have asked of me. JUST STOP RESISTING AND FIGHTING WITH ME ABOUT IT!!! I don't know why you do that. You're so funny to watch.

I'm funny to watch?

Yup. Your soul knows where it's going and your mind is fighting/struggling. It's funny to watch.

Glad I can humor you so!

Lennie sent me this email a year after her discovery.

I was one of the ones who didn't get it at first on how to have a conversation with upstairs. Because of your encouragement and patience I learned. I have a journal full of such conversations now. WONDERFUL stuff just falls from my fingertips!!!!!! When I listen to the god voice, my life works!!! Thanks again!—Lennie

Ah Lennie, I'm ripe with gratitude! So much thanks to you, my dear.

Babysteps was one more person that blessed me with her transition. Pay attention to the timely computer problems. We create those obstacles, you know!

Babysteps/Huntsville/AL

Hi Llovit. ...I apologize for not answering the questions ...Part has to do with computer problems, part has to do with some personal dramas I am undergoing right now—making it very hard for me to focus ...And part has to do with my ego. I am having a hard time discerning whether or not it is my ego or God talking to me. My messages just aren't clear and I still have so much FEAR that I am dealing with. I don't want to hold up any progress on your book so I am going to have to decline any further participation.

> Llovit: Want to tap into your inner god, Babysteps? Want to walk through that fear? You are the one I want in this book, if you do. The questions are irrelevant right now. What would be so beneficial to the readers is to watch how someone walks through fear to the other side. Your struggles will be the reader's struggles. They will think, "If she can do this, maybe I can, too."
>
> Don't worry about holding up the book's progress. It's a moot point. Your part of this book will be a personal struggle to overcome these fears. Commitment to this process is essential, however. Here is what I would like, Babysteps. You write, write, write. Expressing your feelings about this is paramount in helping others. Even if you don't have anything to say about this, you write about feeling frustrated (or whatever) about not having anything to say. Send it to me. I will ask you your own questions to answer.
>
> If you find that the fear is too great, and you just simply CANNOT continue, then I will use nothing. If you DO continue and work through your fears on tapping into your god-self, you will have done a fabulous service to you and the majority of the readers. Your first question, if you choose this mission, is: "What is the fear that I feel whenever I sit down to hear, god?"

You are right—this is exactly what I need right now! I will do this for myself, for you, and for every other one trying too hard and getting nowhere. Thank you for your patience and understanding with me! I am glad to help!

Llovit: Fabulous. Looking forward to your first answer!!

Ok...I was compelled to write as soon as I got my baby to bed—so here it is: What is the fear that I feel whenever I sit down to hear God?

I fear that it is my ego talking and not God and I know that my ego doesn't have all the answers. I fear that I am fooling myself—that I am answering my own questions with what I think I want to hear. I fear that I am not worthy of God talking to me—I have denied and ignored him all these years. I fear that I will be judged by God for my past ways.

I fear that I will have to let down my guard to hear God speak. I fear that I will have to LISTEN. I fear that I won't like the messages that I receive, that they will make me uncomfortable. I fear that I will have to CHANGE upon hearing God speak to me. I fear that I will have to LOVE and do not feel that I am worthy of LOVE. I fear that to talk directly to God would be the end of my quest to find "the truth" and this quest has been the point of my existence.

Llovit: So you think listening to god will change your whole life? What if it doesn't? What if hearing now and then is just icing on the cake? A fun thing to do? And who cares if it's just your ego? Take this as a fun experiment and maybe nothing will happen, anyway. So, nobody is watching right now. Ask this question: "God, are you there?" What would god say if s/he were there? Just for fun.

Ok—here is my response—from my ego ...excuse the goofiness ...I guess it was just the mood I was in.

God, are you there?

Yes, I am always here. It is YOU who is sometimes not here. So, Babysteps, are you here?

Yes God, I am here.

Good, I have been waiting for you! What can I do for you?

Well, for starters, you could make it easier to talk to you!

How can I make it any easier to talk to me? You don't have to pick up a phone, turn on a computer, even lift a finger, nor say a word. Simply open your heart and here I am.

Ah, but the trick is opening my heart!

Yes that is the trick. Let's see it.

See what?

See your trick. Let's see you open your heart — that should be a good one.

Well, I don't know how!

Don't know how? Then how could we be having this conversation?

WE aren't. You are just my ego!

Yes, I am just your ego. I am also your favorite pen you just happened to have found a few minutes ago, that purring cat sitting next to you, your sleeping baby, the guy on the news, your neighbor....

Ok, ok, now I KNOW you are my ego 'cause your examples are so bad!

So are you going to show me the trick?

I don't know the trick- I just picked up a pen and started writing.

That's a pretty good trick if you ask me....but who am I to say? I am just your ego.

If you hadn't picked up on it, Babysteps was actually talking to upstairs rather than her ego, like she thought. Babysteps flourished in this skill. Man, these examples warm my soul.

Here are some other great crossover conversations.

Skeeter

I had a quick but profound conversation with God this morning. I was busy doing laundry and cleaning the house thinking about why it is that my hunger to read all things spiritual is so insatiable. I asked out loud, "What am I looking so hard for in all of these books?"

I remember this vividly ...I was hanging up a pair of pants when I heard a voice as clear and loud as if it was spoken from a person standing right next to me.

"What ever you are searching for in these books that you keep buying, is inside of you right now and always has been. Look within and read and remember what is in you now."

I stopped in my tracks and looked behind me almost expecting someone to be there. It was so profound and joyful that I wanted to cry. I knew at that moment that I had just had a short but sweet conversation with God.

Jimmy L/Denver/CO/USA

I decided to just write, like they say. Just keep the pen moving and not allow any time to think about what I am writing. I did this and low and behold, God came through.

Without thinking and just writing whatever comes into my head I have no idea what I'm tapping in to here, if anything, by random thoughts. Feelings. Allow the feelings to be there accept them and identify them to the utmost state of flourishing. This will set you free.

I didn't separate the voices out on this one. Can you find what part of the above paragraph is upstairs talking? In case you didn't catch it, upstairs came through from the word "Feelings..." to the end. Can you see the slight change in focus?

Jack Aarron/USA

I am back, I am back, I am back, and I am so sorry that it took me so long to get back.

Jack, honestly, you and I have been communicating between these conversations. Do you think that this is the only way that you and I have conversations?

No, but I feel you now, so much! I feel you!!! I know that you are right, though. You are with me at other times. I have felt guilty, as if I have let you down by not having these conversations with you.

Now you know better Jack. You know that you are in no way 'required' to have these conversations with me! I think what you are feeling is that you were fearful that you stopped believing these conversations were real, could that be it?

But I feel you.

You never had the doubting feeling?

Very momentarily.

Why? I ask that in a sincere manner.

I have no idea. But the more I think about it, the more ridiculous it sounds to me that I would have any doubt. The conversations that we have are so inspiring, and I feel so close to you. I love you, and I thank you God, creator of all that is seen and unseen, for everything. I thank you for helping me, and for helping my family and just everything! You are in my life, and I know it.

Wow, does that feel good?

Yes, it does.

Certainly you don't have to thank me. It is thanks enough for me to see that you are viewing some of your irrational fears as irrational. I love you too, Jack Aarron.

You know it, but I got hired on full time finally. That relieves a lot of stress on me, I think.

Do you like the job?

I like it. It probably will not be my lifetime career, but I like it.

What will be your lifetime career?

Hard question for me to answer. I love screenwriting.

We have discussed this before, Jack Aarron. Shall we go over it again?

No. I know what will be said.

Why do you choose not to act, then, on your truest feelings? Surely you know that is what benefits you most.

I love talking with you! You get my mind working so well. I feel that I am headed in that direction. I really do. I sent a pitch for an idea for a script to someone today. That is like one of those first step kind of things. I have been writing, more and more. So, it's like the opportunity is resembling a foundation of a building. It's there, now you (meaning me) just have to build the rest. Or you can leave it sit there.

Which, of course, would be a waste.

Indeed it would be a waste. Thank you for pointing that out. I have never thought of it that way. It would be a waste for me to enjoy doing something like this, to do all that I have done so far, and never take it anywhere. But I want to get back to you.

What about me?

I just appreciate everything. I want to do something for you.

You are every moment of every day, Jack Aarron. Don't you see that by now? You've read it, we have spoken of it. I am experiencing myself through you!

So by carrying out myself normally, I am, in a way, doing something for you?

You and I are one. When you do something for me, you are doing something for yourself. When you do something for yourself, you are doing something for me. It all works together.

I see.

And when I do something for myself, it could be said that I am doing something for you. When I do something for you ... get the picture?

Yes, I do totally! This helps SO MUCH!!!! You just don't know. Well, you do. But I can't express how much this helps talking to you tonight. I will not forget this conversation!!! I will print it off, and keep it with me or something.

You do that, JackAarron!

I love you!

I love you too!

Irishmossey

I, too, was moved to start writing. I wanted to post, but I feared, quite honestly, to share it. I'm following Llovit's lead on this. Here was my first writing (and can give you a much truer notion of where I really am in the Oneness).

I'm pissed off--tired of this feeling of "can't move"-both physically and emotionally. So bored—can't muster ANY motivation to do anything. Driving Mossy crazy. He's driving me crazy. And I don't feel comfortable speaking to anybody about this. Please help me to understand. No, no, not understand—I have that in my head. But even that has not caused motivation to change.

Nothing...I hear nothing....

Clear the channel.

Clear it of what?

The noise you put there.

What kind of noise? Nothing...I hear nothing....WHAT KIND OF NOISE????

Your fear and wow do you have a lot of that.

What do I fear?

Fear-you even fear fear, for one thing.

What else?

Yourself—you won't let go and BE yourself. Do you even know who you are? Your tears tell me you want to remember, but you refuse to let yourself. Why do you choose to suffer like this, my child? Your fears are many, circling around you.

How do I stop this madness?

Stop fearing. Stop it-right now—choose different.

This is all gobbilty goop to me on a personal level—I'm pissed.

I know you are. Why is it gobbilty goop for you?

Because in my heart I don't believe it. My head does—my heart doesn't.

WRONG. Your head has no idea. Your heart longs for what it already knows to be truth.

How can I change this?

Be something different.

I'm hitting the "Post Message" button—and boy this is hard for me ...here goes ...click.

LittleSoul/Anadarko/OK

Well, I was asked to write down my conversation with you so it could be put in a book. This will be hard for two reasons. First, because the communications flow too fast, and second because I mostly converse with you in thoughts and feelings.

Well, I'll try to go slow for you. If you really noticed, you'd realize you have a few words in with those thoughts and feelings. The thing is you pay more attention to thoughts and feelings. I am encouraging this since words can't describe one speck of what feelings and thoughts can. People will understand.

Understand what?

You may not use the most descriptive words, seeing as though you usually pay attention to feelings.

Okay. Well, as you know, no one I tell about all this communication stuff believes me. I guess it's because they don't have the same feeling of completeness as me.

In actuality, they don't have a feeling of completeness at all. There are times when they feel peace, but this is far different. What you, and many others have, is a feeling of true enlightenment. You are well on your way towards mastery.

Your individualized soul chooses this in this particular human life. Every different mix chooses a different life. Since we are all one, every other aspect of me feels every experience of every other aspect of me. The soul knows every part of itself. You know what's happening to your hand when it's smashed. You know what happened to your toe when you stubbed it. They are two separate things, and yet a part of the same thing. You know what both of them went through. It's the same way with the soul.

I love it when you make analogies like that!

Well, sometimes I get lucky...

I guess whenever you choose!

Yes!

Could you give me a little more elaborate explanation about time? We've felt this before but many people still ask, confused. Many ask what is meant by "What is happening now is all that ever happened and all that ever will happen".

Yes. Well, since the present is all there is, and past and future are made up imaginings, this very moment is all that ever will happen and all that ever did happen. But wait! It just changed! This moment is all that ever happened and all that ever will happen, until it changes. Then, that moment will be the only moment that ever happened and ever will happen, until that changes!

Yes, I think that will help a little more. Thank you!

You're surely welcome, my little soul...

You know ...this stuff isn't very personal, and that is this dialogue's intention.

It is?

Yeah. I was asked to hold a personal dialogue.

But don't you see that this is all personal? Don't you see that the very act of you asking me questions is personal in itself?

But the time question wasn't mine. It was for to help others understand.

Other parts....Of you? You chose it from me, and that's personal as it is. You could ask me how many people are in Washington State right now, and the answer would be for everyone in China. It would be a very personal question because you asked your own soul this question.

I understand.

That's nice. I sure as hell wasn't going to explain it again!

Ha, ha, ha.

Yeah.

I don't really know what to talk to you about. I guess concentrating on the communication makes it harder.

Yes, but it doesn't have to be. When you aren't concentrating on your thinking, your thoughts are free, out of your control because you don't care what comes through. You are expecting the thoughts to come through. Don't expect. Accept.

Okay. I am accepting my thoughts coming through.

Yes, and now you have a whole paragraph from me. Accept more, and you could have pages. Even books!

Yes. I understand that.

Llovit/WA/USA

At one stage, I didn't tap in to upstairs for quite some time. When connecting once again, after staying away, sometimes it's difficult to get clear communication right away. This conversation is one of those times. You will see how some of the words and phrases seem disconnected at first, with words not making a lot of sense. But as the "rustiness" wears off, the clarity begins to emerge. I cannot even remember what prompted this chat question in the first place.

What do you make of my fears?

It is good that you recognize them as fears. What you feel and what you do are two different things and if one is to replace the other, then a change of habit is necessary. In your works, you have learned to let go and see what I have to say and then take that information and sort it through. Is this any different? Are you not paying attention to this message because you do not want to hear it?

I am afraid of interfering with it. I want to be a clear channel and am putting my mind aside so you can come through.

This is a good attempt at getting what you want. I will just talk and you can determine where any of this needs to go in your life. As we get further into this, your message will be clearer. Now, you have asked a question. I can answer in one way, but would appreciate an answer in another way.

Okay, I can channel or I can let go and allow my fingers to do the walking. Which should I do?

When you think of circumstances beyond your control, you find that there are many facets to each circumstance. This is to your choosing. Don't make too much out of it. Do it each way and see where it leads you. Also knowing where you want to go.

I am most comfortable just doing this as in a written conversation. Is that okay? And I want something profound so I can be sure I am not making this up.

Profound, huh? You ask for tough information to appease your fears. Just flow with it and the tough info will come out, as will the easy info.

Okay, you have ten minutes. I will commit to not being distracted for ten minutes. That's all I can commit to right at this minute.

Good enough. The question is about equality. When there were humans in the first days of human existence, all were equal in all aspects. Humans were like us, all loving, all knowing, all connected. Then it was decided to have the veil of forgetfulness cover all humans so god could experience his creation. In this forgetting of who and what they were, humans inherently assumed that they were less than. Without that knowledge and feeling of connectedness, a part of each human knew there was something missing inside. When the veil was draped on you, and your knowledge and soul connection was hampered, there was a vein of misunderstanding. All of a sudden you did not know who you were, where you were going, or why you came here. This meant the veil worked perfectly.

A child knows not how to walk but has the inherent instinct to do so through no logical conclusion. The child does not understand why he wants to walk, he just wants to and will do so, regardless of his ability. It is programmed in each child to WANT to walk. This is called evolution. Every human has this inherent within him. Every human wants to remember what he once knew. The veil is more like a blanket as there is no seeing through it. There is only a tug of war to get the blanket off. Most humans will achieve that goal, as most children will one day walk. It is not possible for a person to not achieve the goal of remembering who they are, feeling that connection and being at one with all others. As every child will learn to walk in his own time, every human will evolve in his own time. Some will take 500 lifetimes, some will take two.

In this age of acceleration, the urgency of evolving is known at some level in each human. There is a push in the universe for those who are to evolve to do so, and those that will not evolve will go the opposite way. The earth will soon begin anew. The evolved beings will inherit the earth. The weak, as some say. Weak only in that evolved beings do not choose to fight over anything. They create. If things are not at their liking, they create another situation where it is. One that is better, more to their liking. Evolved beings do not hold on to fear. They let go. Is my time up?

That was thirteen minutes. I have to rest now.

Llovit/WA/USA

Due to an upcoming company buy out with my job, I decided it would be best to move closer to work. At the time I was living 75 miles away from the job, working only 40 hours a week. This new buy out and ownership would require me to work 72-80 hours a week. Making the decision I would stay with the job, I began searching diligently for a much closer, affordable home on acreage for me and my animal family (2 horses, 1 mule, 1 donkey, 1 dog, 1 cat). My days off were filled with 1-2 hour drives into the city, in all directions, to look at perspective homes. On my working days, searching the newspapers, soliciting rental property managers, and engaging in phone calls, filled much of my time. I was becoming exhausted.

After a full two months of searching for a home, I wasn't much further along than when I started. Owning a dog seemed to be the biggest problem for many landlords. Nevertheless, I forged onwards. Nothing was going to break up my family, even though my frustration became overwhelmingly high. By now, the company I was working for had already been bought out and changed ownership. The hours and days were increased and looking for a new, closer home was even harder. I was beginning to feel very pressured and exhausted as every spare moment was dedicated to finding this new home for me and my animal family. I finally sat down and had a stress-filled chat with upstairs.

Two months and still nothing materializing. How freaking long does god take? Upstairs, I ask you. Why the hell you taking your own sweet time when every day is added stress for me? Why the hell can't you make this manifest NOW, not 6 months from now? The job changed and still the house didn't manifest. What's wrong with you? Do you enjoy me struggling, stressing? Do you sit back and laugh at me? Like you got the controls over me and my moods? Laughing all the way at me freaking out. Why do you do this to me? You like to see me struggle and stress? Is this FUN for you? Don't you have better things to do? Like helping me manifest a home?

I'm not in your way.

Oh come on now. I am doing my part, here. Sometimes it seems like you aren't helping a bit and there is NO partnership between you and I.

I can see it looks that way to you. But let me assure you I am on your side.

So, what's the problem in finding a home?

(I got a blank. Nothing. No answer.)

What is this NOTHING stuff???? How come I get no answers? Help me, please?

Yes.

That was the end of that chat. When totally stressed out, I usually get very little words from upstairs. However, it seems that when I verbalize it or write down my feelings, I do get quicker action and results from upstairs, even when stressed to the max.

Not long thereafter, I found a really nice home on 5 acres where I was able to have all of my family, including me, in one location. This was a 20 year dream come true. The home was even larger, more modern than I ever thought I could afford or deserved to have. It was in the town I wanted, the perfect distance away from work. I guess not all was lost!

In the years that followed this conversation I have grown and learned the intricacies of understanding how to get what I want. It is not all about action, about fighting, about wrestling something to the ground as if to kill it, it is about relaxing, letting go, being in that happy state, and knowing all things will work out for the best. Of course there is more to it than that, but I now can see that my emotional state when this was written was actually blocking the answer, the home, from materializing.

Chapter 4
Who Can Have These Chats?

I would like all readers to take full advantage of the valued ideas, insightful perspectives, and high thought answers that fall between the covers of this book. There is such great wisdom on within these pages. It is my desire that you read the profound words presented, try them on for size, notice how the message feels inside, and see if it fits for you. Or, maybe one message will fit and another will not. Regardless of where these words come from, if you resonate with what you read, by all means take it home and wear it fluently. If not, put the words back in the book and continue on!

I was excited to start this question and answer session with the participant pool. They, too, were excited to get going with the first question. I knew that this tapping into the god-self through writing was such a valuable practice, it made me curious why everyone wasn't fluently chatting with upstairs on their own. Therefore, this first question was posed to the participants to address this curiosity. Excited as a racehorse in the starting gate, I sent this first question. And...we were off and running!

> *Question: "Upstairs, if anyone can communicate with you, why are some people better than others at this? Is there preliminary work that a person should do to better be able to dialog with you?"*

With excited anticipation, soon the answers came rolling in.

Scott/Arizona

All are able to communicate with me. Most are very good at speaking to me and asking for assistance. The problems arise when it comes time to LISTEN to the answers that I have for them. Most of you are looking for an answer that you want to hear, not necessarily what serves you best. Jesus, as well as other Masters, were very good at HEARING me, thus they were walking a more Enlightened path than the masses.

Preliminary work? Yes, you can start by going within. Find your center, your Inner Self as it is. It is then that you will find the Truth you seek. Meditation and inspired readings will guide you. All answers come from within.

Marilyn/Amboy/WA

I talk to you because you believe in me, and are able to hear me on a level which is coming from a pure heart. Let me explain here. Words are so limiting. In using the term pure, I am not comparing it to something as being opposite, or un-pure. Your intention, in communicating with me, is to know and understand more about yourself. In order to do that, you need to be willing to hear anything I might share with you, without judgment, without assumptions, without attachments. You need to be in the moment and clear with your intentions. When you are in this state, I choose to define or describe it as pure, meaning without a lot of other stuff clouding the communication or getting in the way. Like you might consider pure water, or pure love, as being clear without any other stuff contained within. A clear vessel could be another phrase I would choose to use. Becoming a clear vessel. You can actually hear me more than you wish to acknowledge.

I know in this instance you are referring to asking and answering questions and receiving information, in the moment, which you can use. I am god and everything is god, therefore you are god too, and so is there god in all life. So, when you are talking to a friend, having an argument, communicating with your cat, listening to a tree, you are therefore communicating with me, right? I send each of you messages in zillions of different ways, and most of the time you are unaware that they are there; or ....from where they might have come from. You are so focused, still, on an external representation of God. You have a limited way of accepting answers to the questions you ask. You (meaning people in general) still have difficulty saying the words "I am God" and truly feeling this with every cell of your body, taking it in and making it real. When you are able to do this and really believe it, you will know I sing to you daily from every flower, from every tree, from every smile on a face, and from your own reflection in the mirror. Stop and smell the roses because if you listen closely you will hear me singing your name.

SAM/Clinton/Mass

Everyone can hear me if they choose to listen. Those who seek me ...find me. Those who expect me to find them ...are left alone in their own self-created reality ...for I am always there and always have been. Open more than your eyes ...open your soul. Seek to satisfy your soul. Listen to your soul for then you are listening to me. Trust your soul for then you are trusting me.

It is not hard ...it never was. It is wonderfully and perfectly simple to dialog with me. Allow it to happen. Be aware of everything, for I am in everything. Ask a question and listen. Turn on the radio ...is there an answer to your question in the song that is playing? ...Don't dismiss or ignore the people around you ...they may hold your answer. Look into your self, get to know your soul ...for it is your best friend and will never let you down ...if you hold no expectations. If you can not hear me ...then you are not listening.

LittleSoul/Anadarko/OK

First of all, a person does not have to do anything. There are no "shoulds" or "should nots". Secondly, there is no work. Everything you do is through your choice because you desire it and that is the only reason. Souls do exactly what they choose. If they choose not to hear me at all, then so shall it be. If they choose for me to hear them completely, then so shall that be.

There is a cycle that a soul goes through, a growing cycle. In this cycle the soul grows to know more and more experiences using relativity. It experiences this in what you call physical life. Now, let's say the cycle has just started for a particular soul. This soul has forgotten its past experiences and is far from mastery in physical life. This soul chooses to experience everything it possibly can before it reaches mastery once again in physical life. So it includes the experiences of not knowing my true presence because that is one of the ever possible experiences. There are many, many more. Now, some souls choose to be more elaborate in their experiences than others. They may choose to experience two very similar lives. They may like a particular life so much that they choose to live the same life over again!

This is why there are variations in physical consciousness' closeness to me. They end their cycle at different times because they choose different soulic lives to lead. Some start their cycle over sooner than others. They may even stay at mastery for every physical life from now on if they choose it, although it is very unlikely. The soul gets and does exactly what it chooses. This is the base answer to your question. If it chooses to be less evolved, so shall it joyfully be. If it chooses mastery faster than the rest, so shall it perfectly be.

The thing is that you similaritize physical life so closely to soulic life. You think since in the relative world you go from a beginner level to an intermediate level, it must be that way for the non-relative world— far from it. Relativity and non-relativity are very completely different things, so this causes completely different outcomes, feelings, and situations; but this is perfect and I love you for it. You are living your life the way you choose, so shall it be!

In what forms do you communicate with us?

I communicate with you in only and all the forms in which each of you wish me to. It depends on your beliefs. A Catholic believes his god can only communicate with him through the priest.

There is no place I cannot communicate to you. There is nothing that can keep us from communicating. The only thing that does keep our communications stalled is your (society) own ignorance. Many of you believe that my powers can create a world, a universe, life; but I cannot communicate with my creations? Why couldn't I? And for those who believe I just don't do it, why wouldn't I? Why wouldn't I choose to send you my messages, to help you through when you are having trouble? You chose to experience physical life yourselves, to experience relativity, but you did not choose to leave me completely, to separate totally from me. Who would desire to separate from their own creator? Do you want to completely separate from your parents when you move out of the house? Most of you don't.

You want help along the way whenever you desire it. For those of you who do choose to stray from me in physical life, that is perfect! You choose to do this in order to see what it's like to live on your own. The children of the parents will always forgive them some time. They will always be ready to love them once again, whether it is after their parents have moved onward, or if they are still in this particular physical form.

I love it when you make those analogies!

Me too, for I love what you love. I am what you are. I have created what you will choose!

How do we know it is you talking?

How could you not know? I love how your society always seems to resist the obvious. When it even slaps you in the face, you ignore it. You see hints that your loved one has left, who has changed form, to show you that they are still here, watching over you. Do you see it? I tell you, if your consciousness were out here observing your planet as a whole, you'd be laughing.

You know that it is me communicating because I am the feeling which calls itself me. Every feeling is me! The thing is, it's hard for some to tell feelings from thoughts of fear. Every feeling is what your truth is. Your truth is:

- Never fear because it doesn't really exist.
- Whatever fear you have is not from me because I only communicate love.
- All thoughts of love are from me because all love is natural.

Fear is from those people controlling you. It is from those who don't truly know love, or they wouldn't need fear for you to do what they want. If they truly knew love, everything you did would be what they wanted, so they wouldn't have the desire to change you.

In summary, everything communicated in love is from me. And every other feeling that tells you it's me is also me because your feelings never lie to you. You just have to be sensitive to know if they are your feelings. Love is all there is. I am what is not, but I only communicate what is. And that's not changing!

Thank you so much for that. I am truly grateful that you are this way. I don't know what I would do if you were really a fearing God.

Well, you don't have to ever believe the illogical....

JofromAlaska

Hi God.

Hi, Jo.

Well, here I am, bringing a question from Llovit. Don't think I have ever come "bringing" a question before. Except maybe inside my own head—sort of unformed. So, is it okay?

Is it?

Well, I thought it was worth a try. Hmmm...the question?

> *"God, if anyone can hear you, why are some people better than others at this? Is there some preliminary work that a person should do to better be able to dialog with you?"*

Well, what did you do, Jo?

Well, first I had a strong desire to know You. To know Your thoughts, and Your truths, and Your Directions for me.

Yes, and then?

Well, maybe it was first, but I wanted to be able to "Listen" and "Hear" you. It all started with a book about listening to god given to me by my Pastor over 30 years ago. That really got me started.

Yes, a while back, wasn't it?

It was about 1971 or so.

And then?

Well, I think I was really drawn to books wherein You were speaking to people. I really liked hearing what You had to say. It seemed like that was what was essential. And I think that the more I heard what you had to say to others, the more I knew how you talked, and What You had to say. I sort of got to know you.

And I realized that there was a good reason for the red letters in the Bible, for Your/Jesus's words. And I wondered why they didn't do that with the Old Testament, so that it would be easy to find Your words there. And one day, I got a Rainbow Bible—and they had Your words in capitals -everywhere throughout the entire Bible. I just loved it.

I also found many other books written by people, telling what You said to them. And I learned about the Friends, (or Quakers) some of whom spend an hour a day just "waiting on the Lord" for direction. And who have meetings wherein nothing is said except to share words that are being heard from you. I would love to attend such a meeting. I did try to spend time alone listening—but I soon lost track and got distracted. Don't think I ever did hear much in that way.

But I attend a Catholic Charismatic Bible Study, wherein time is spent awaiting words from You. And I further learned how to hear you. We were encouraged that if we did not share what we heard, that You could share it through others, or that, as it says in the Bible, "even the rocks will shout". And I did not want to deny you, so I learned to share what I heard—and was amazed how when I was slow to do so, someone else would share the exact same word I was getting up my gumption to share. That was real confirming for me.

Now I still like to read and see what You are saying to others, to see if it is similar to what You are saying to me—if it sounds the same. And it almost always does!

And?

And, I am very happy and feel your words are very important—more important than anyone else's words, and so they are the words I prefer to hear.

Then why don't you talk to me more?

Because I get all wound up in living my life, and doing it my way. Or I am busy or in a hurry, and just don't even think about You. And when I do, I know you are patient and loving and that I can take my time and come to you when the desire is adequate for me to spend time calming down and becoming peaceful enough to really concentrate and pay attention. To put You first.

Aha! That does take you time and effort, doesn't it?

I suppose if I did it more often, it might become easier.

You do?

Well, yes. I think that might be true.

Do you realize that you are spending most of the time talking, Jo?

Well, I just get so full and excited with this subject. And to think that Llovit is interested in it, too!

Yes, it is nice to know you care. (And she does, too.)

I always care, but I am not good at keeping it in my mind due to Attention Deficit Disorder.

Your "you"-ness?

My "me"-ness. Thank you for loving me just that way.

How could I not? Now ...the questions. I think there were 2 of them.

> *"If anyone can hear you, why are some people better at it than others?"*

Well, I think you have answered that.

Because they care more?

Heart's desire. You are not letting me speak as much as usual, Jo. You are feeling self-conscious, knowing this will be shared?

Yes.

Second question—

> *"Is there preliminary work to be able to better dialogue."*

I think I have mostly answered that. Except to mention, that for me, I do not hear a voice, I more or less hear a thought. And it is much easier for me to keep track of what is being said, and to keep focused when I am writing it down—like in my journal, or typing it, like now.

Well, you have pretty much answered the questions for me.

Yes, my answers.

And maybe more than yours?

Tiaka/Japan

No one is better than another at listening to God. We all have the equally wondrous ability to converse with god. When you deny this, you give your ability of insight to another. Whole religions have been based on this denial. This is not necessarily a bad thing, as you can be pleasantly surprised when you re-establish contact with the god within. We are all loving, spiritual beings of and from god. Quiet times and time spent in nature can help us communicate.

Yet don't be disheartened, as all is, of, and from God. And everything in your life is a reminder of who you wish to be right now. If you feel nothing is being said, then perhaps you are living your dreams and creating anew your very life each day. This being is the most powerful form of creation. It is you communicating directly to the earth. You have thus opened the channel from the source to earth. You are being God! Deny all you like, yet enjoy every moment. And remember god has an infinite array of methods for communicating. What you see, hear, feel, smell, taste and intuitively know, is all from God. God is communicating constantly. Sleepwalk if you must, but try not to be angry if you are violently awoken. Of course you may just be shaken softly. You choose and enjoy. Have fun and remember, we all have this ability to converse with God. It is held back from none, save only if you block it yourself.

Jay/Lismore/NSW/Australia

They listen. This is achieved by letting go of thoughts, feelings and emotions. Some people like to hang on because of fear. However, once they realize that I will protect them, they can fully surrender to my will.

Holy Toledo, my brain is swimming after those answers! Hearing the wisdom in these answers, this is going to be a fantastic ride. Can the human mind to fully grasp the vastness of how things really are? Nevertheless, we have more questions to answer and a purpose to fulfill.

Chapter 5
Who Are You, Upstairs?

I thought it was appropriate, as well as essential, to let the group answer this question about who they were actually talking to when accessing that special place inside we call god or upstairs.

Question: "Who am I speaking with? Are you the ultimate god of everything? An angel? My own personal, spiritual guide? In essence, who are you upstairs?"

LittleSoul/Anadarko/OK

My dearest and lovely Llovit. Why can't I be all three and more? I am that which is your highest self. I am that little voice in your head when you are doing something that may harm you. I am the things that are, and I am also the things that aren't. I am everything. I am the everything that you are because we are all one. You are everything as well. When I talk to you, I can be your imagination, your conscious, your thoughts, your feelings, anything that you use for communicating to others, anything that you use for showing emotion, anything that you use which shows the difference and relationship between you and every other wonderfully living thing on this delightful earth. I always love you. I am love. I am the loving you. I am the fearing you, although it is something you created. I am. I AM!

Lennie/OH/USA

Ok God, now that you are here, will you answer Llovit's questions?

Sure will.

Who are you?

I am all that I am.

Sounds like a bible quote. Really, who are you?

I am all that I am. You have no words that can describe who I am.

Ok, are you the ultimate god of everything.

Everything that you know to be so—your understanding. Yes, but I m not the only god.

You're not?

No, there are lots of beings such as myself.

Stop. I don't want to hear this.

You don't?

No.

Then why ask me?

Because Llovit asked me to.

Why do you think I asked Llovit to have you ask me?

I don't know. Can we just let this one go for the time being? I don't want to hear that answer.

There you go again—resisting the very things I've brought into your life. Stop resisting me.

Oh God, I really don't want to have this discussion just now. Can we please table that question?

Your wish is my command.

Are you an angel?

No. What you call angels is really me. Some folks just can't handle—choose not to handle—that I will be there if they ask. So they make up this nice story about an angel. But please know, it is me.

Are you my own personal spiritual guide?

What do you think?

Yes, I think you are my own personal guide. That you are a personal guide to each and every one of us.

Bingo! The key is to listen.

Marilyn/Amboy/WA

I am you, I am everything. You might desire to label me so that you could confine my essence to a place and time, to an "is-ness" or an "is-not-ness". I am everything you see and I am also nothing you can see without turning inside. Life is what? Can you separate anything out that is not life? What is a tomato and what is not? What part of life did not participate in creating the tomato? You tell me. You create the label for me, and then desire to find a package on which to put it. The divine paradox—I am everything and yet without form or definition. You can never catch me and yet I am always with you. I will not become your definition of myself. You become a definition of me.

DJS/NB/Canada

You are speaking with the eternal light, the infinite spirit, and your equal. I am the ultimate thought the ultimate word, the endless cycle of love with you and all universal beings. We are one in kind— currently being of light. Angels are an illusion. I am not that— although I am your guardian god with you when the need arises. I am not a spiritual guide. I could not be; for you/we guide ourselves through all time and space. We are now and have been for eons. I am your soul. You feel that now, don't you? We are One.

JofromAlaska

Hi God. Well, here we are again. Thank goodness for Llovit or I would probably not be dialoguing with you at all or very much lately. I have my friend on the phone. Is it okay if she joins us?

Of course, Jo. Try it however you like. See if it works.

And the question begins with: "Who am I speaking with?" Or, to be more proper English grammar-wise, "With whom am I speaking?"

If you don't know by now...

Yes, but for Llovit's book. For others.

Yes for all. I hear "I am" rattling around in your brain. You want me to come up with something clever.

Yes.

Okay, "I Am" not a trained seal!

You do not jump and leap at my command—do not like being tested?

I love people coming to me and truly and sincerely wanting to know about me and to "know" me. That is what I love. And yes, I do not like being tested just for show. I Am that I Am. You know that, Jo.

Yes I do. Next..

"Are you the ultimate god of everything?"

I Am.

"An angel?"

Some people see/hear/think me that way. How do you know me? That is how I Am.

"My own personal spirit guide?"

That is who I would like to be, and who I think you desire me to be, sometimes when you aren't busy "rather-do-it-myself-ing".

"In essence, who are you Upstairs?"

In essence, you just read a passage in CWG [Conversations with God] Book Two[1] that struck you as true, yes?

Yes. Should I quote it here?

If you like.

---

[1]Walsch, Neale Donald. <u>Conversations With God, Book 2</u>. 1997. Hampton Roads Publishing. Charlottesville, NC.

It/you said, "I am the wind which rustles your hair. I am the sun which warms your body." You are my Creator, the one who made me and loves me just the way I am.

Yes, I am your creator, creator of all. Yes, Jo, of all. And I do love you all, more than you can or ever will know.

Enough to let your son die for me.

Yes that, and so much more that you shall never know.

Never?

Not until you do.

In the book, You went on to say "I am the rain which dances on your face." And that is quite a lot here in the rain forest.

Yes, "I am the beginning of your first thought, the end of your last".

You created me—were there at my birth.

At your creation, you were my thought to begin with!

You will be there at my death.

Always, always, Jo. "I am the idea which sparked your most brilliant moment."

You spark all my moments.

Remember me.

How could I not?

Indeed.

Jay/Lismore/NSW/Australia

You are speaking with the one who knows you. You are speaking with the emperor of time. I am god to some, to others a simple thought. I am the master of time, universe, light, and love. I come to you with reassurance that all is in my domain. I am the one who comforts you. I am the one who guides you, and I am the one who speaks to you when you don't listen. I am that I am. I am the alpha and omega, beginning and the end. I am different things to all on the universe and far beyond.

When you see with your eyes, do you see with your eyes? When you hear with your ears, do you hear with your ears? When you feel, do you feel with your heart, soul, or hands? When you can let go of earthly attachments and answer the above, then you will know me exactly as I am.

> *Llovit: Sorry to be so dense. This sounds very poetic, but I do not really understand the meaning. Can you explain this in a more simplistic way?*

You are not dense. The writer has a poetic streak that she uses to get in touch with me and she can turn off her own thoughts. She has not yet quite mastered stepping out of the way, only through poetry can she do this. I will explain. Do you see with your eyes or do you see with your mind, or do you see with a knowing (an understanding)? Do you hear with your ears or can you hear me by turning off the thoughts in your head? Do you feel with your heart, soul, or hand; or do you feel with a knowing, a sense? You ask what I am? I am many things to many individuals. I am spirit, a vibration that takes many forms. What way one will see me, another will see me a different way. So, who is right, who is wrong? The truth for an individual lies in their perception. No two see the same. If you want to know who I am, I am inside of you and I am all around in everything. If you want to know me, you only have to close your eyes, mind, and turn off your thoughts and listen. That is where you will find me, that is where I will be.

SAM/Clinton/Mass

I Am Everything not of everything. I am you, I am me ...the alpha, the omega, the up and the down. I will guide you if you ask. I am your best friend. In essence, I am the essence of everything. I am the purity of what you taste, what you hear, what you smell, what you touch, what you see, what you know. You want to classify me as some thing, and I tell you that I am all things, all things ...you ...me ...the earth and the sky ...all things being one thing ...ME. In essence, I am the whole. You are me, if only you would remember. In essence, you are me. In essence, you are the whole. Simple, perfectly simple.

Chapter 6
Why Aren't Some Hearing You?

In the responses sent to me, I'd occasionally run across answers which seemed obvious to me to be logical/opinion/ego-self answers rather than that deeper wisdom from upstairs. When I responded and asked the submitters to dig deeper into themselves and find that inner connection to upstairs, one submitter questioned as to why their words were 'not good enough' for the book. Another submitter suggested if god is all things, then god is ego as well. And that ego-self answers were just as valid as the deeper wisdom of god-self answers. Plus, one other person questioned, "Who are you to judge where the words come from? That would be like you were judging God."

This questioning threw me for a loop, as I was unprepared for a challenge of this sort. I didn't seem to have difficulty deciphering ego-self words from god-self words, but apparently others did. The good that came out of this was a dilemma, and an important question to pose to the participants.

> Question: "Here we have people whom desire to have a dialog with you—yet, they either cannot or choose not, for one reason or another. Please give some advice, practical steps, or wisdom to help these people be able/willing to converse with you."

Jay/Lismore/NSW/Australia

People sometimes fear, people sometimes do not listen, people sometimes mistake what is written because of their thoughts and feelings. Do not think this is you, you are doing what I would like you to do. The writer is ready to answer, her thoughts are gone, her heart is opened, and she can hear me—so let us begin.

They do not dialog with me because they do not listen, they do all the conversing. If they would just stop and take time to take a breath they would hear me, see me, in all of the glory that I am. People sometimes block because of fear and guilt. They may desire to communicate with me and yet they hold back. They do not surrender. If they would open up and listen, let love flow into their hearts, and stop their thoughts for all but a moment, then they would hear. One of the problems for this is the television. So spend a night away from the set and just turn off your brain. Nothing will happen. Only that I will know that you are finally listening to me. And when I know that you do this, you will hear me loud and clear. Please know this, that I do not converse just within a person; I use whatever it takes to get through. Sometimes this will be done through different mediums: books, media, people, nature, sometimes situations, etc. When you know this to be true [it] will be a dawning for the person—like an awakening—and their thoughts will be calmed. For I love all.

Marilyn/Amboy/WA

Mostly this has to do with letting go of fear. Each person is a unique individual and so I respond to each person in a different way. What people want is conformity or a universality, which will lend more weight to the idea that this is all real. Some people are afraid of getting the "wrong" answers, as if such things could occur. They could, of course, have their own filters in place so strongly they hear what they want to hear. They could also hear what they assume or fear I would say. Any and all of these are possibilities. Conversing with god is like conversing with anything and everything else, be it another human being, an animal friend, a tree, a river, or your car. If you really listen to your friend, without any assumptions or judgments getting in the way, in a space of unconditional love, you will usually hear what they are saying. If you don't understand, you can ask for clarification. The same is true of other beings. Being in the moment and really present shows you respect others; the same way you appreciate when others are there in this way for you. So, you can use the same tools in any situation and receive the answers you desire. You need to remain open and humble, without attachments or expectations. Answers can also come in many forms, as you will know. Sometimes, in the midst of your confusion, you have suddenly seen a rainbow. This is a personal sign, meant for you and you know exactly what it means, whenever you see it. Other people would not receive that message and may get something entirely different. So you need not limit yourself, either, to this formal one. The Universe is much more limitless than you imagine, so ask your questions and then stand back and allow the answers to appear in a time and fashion unique unto you. Later, you could put them into words if necessary. Loving you ...(smile) ...God.

SAM/Clinton/Mass

The problem lies in your [Llovit's] expectations. Have none ...and you won't be disappointed. Remember to send your message and send it well. You cannot control how it is then received. You have a goal in mind yet that goal is limited right now. This is a new process for you and for those willing to help. Let it unfold and then see what you have. There are some who write you whom, like yourself, really want this book to come to be ...and it will ...if you let it. Not everyone will be helpful in this process, even if they did sign up. They just might not be at the same level of understanding as you.

Keep your expectations of others low and use what you know in your heart to be useful in writing your book. Originally you had an expectation of how things would go ...You would produce a book of writings ....dialogues ....of others. Bend with the information. There are similarities in some of the responses you received ...those are to be noted. We are all filters of God's word ....some cleaner than others ...Some may try to over think what they are writing in order to sound a certain way, or maybe they are thinking so much with their mind that they are not listening to what's deep inside their soul. Each must go at their own pace.

Don't hold yourself to a strict rule that you will include everything that comes your way. It is self serving to include only those who's message is what you're after ...but to be self serving is a benefit to those who read your book. You want clear consistent messages from God. Neale (Neale Donald Walsch, *Conversations with God, Books*

1,2,3[2]) had only himself as a filter ...you are seeking many ...therefore you are the final filter to send the message you know in your soul to be beneficial to those who will read it. It might be beneficial to those who really want to help you, but are on the wrong track to format a possible page of your future book ...including only those dialogues you found most valuable. This will give the person who really wants to help an idea of exactly what you are looking for.

> *Llovit writes: SAM, one of the things I really would like to do is to help others who say they want to communicate with you, but fear or blockage is in the way. Should I attempt to give them direction or a push, or should I just allow all to reach this communication level at their own time?*

Do they see it as fear or blockage or is that what you surmise from their responses. If it is they who know they are afraid, or they themselves experience blockage, then it may serve them well to express what they are going through publicly with all those who are with you ...Then ...wouldn't it be interesting to see what advice we all could give these people? ...Wouldn't it be interesting to see similarities in the advice ...proving that the advice is coming from one source ...me? When several ask the same question ...I always have the same answer ...any variance stems from the fact that we are all filters. Find the similar answers and you can be sure they come from me ...You will know it in your soul!

On the other hand ...if you are sensing that there is fear or blockage in your responses ...then you are probably correct ...But if these people "don't get it" ...you can push or nudge all you want. But until they come into awareness on their own ...you will not get what you are seeking, because. ...they don't know what they are seeking. No expectations. If you keep them in the loop ...if they want to ...if they seek to understand...they will. Keep posting your questions to all whom have signed up ...focus on the similarity in the responses for these are pure. Post the pure and keep going. Those who desire the

---

[2] Walsch, Neale Donald. Conversations with God, Book 1. 1995. GP Putnam's Sons. NY NY.
Walsch, Neale Donald. Conversations with God Book 2 and Book 3. 1997. Hampton Roads Publishing. Charlottesville, NC.

purity of my message ...eventually will ...and you never know who will or who won't ...so don't disregard anyone who signed up. But remain forever patient ...it will all come together ...if you let it be.

JofromAlaska

Hi Llovit, from Jo and God. First I want to say, I think your efforts are outstanding, and this is the best thing I have been involved in. I felt very privileged to receive the answers to previous questions. I will admit that this is very weighty, and I have not yet read all of them. Although I answered the first two questions quickly, it is a really emotional experience. Sometimes I can absorb a lot at a sitting. Other times only a tiny bit.

It seems easy for me to dialogue with God and I wonder if I am really dialoguing as deeply as I might—or as others are. But this is how He and I talk now, and so this is what I have to share. So this is what I am sharing. I do believe that when I spent more time dialoguing with Him, or really took myself apart to do so, that perhaps I did less of the talking and He more (i.e., I listened more and more deeply). But over time we sometimes just smile and that is our entire conversation—like old friends. But perhaps friends who are no longer spending enough time together, or enough energy on that time. Perhaps I am too casual.

Anyway [to Llovit], I think you are doing absolutely marvelously!!!!! I think your questions have been just perfect. I have long wanted to help others be able to experience their own ability to dialog and I think the answers should be extremely helpful.

Doing it (listening and dialoguing) with my prayer group was very supportive in learning to listen and know when I was hearing—and what other people were hearing.

> Llovit: Jo, I'm a bit frustrated with only receiving answers from about half who signed up for this project.

Listen, Llovit, please don't be discouraged. Life seems to be very much like that, nowadays. Somehow people's spoken intentions seldom seem to produce actions for more than a portion of the people speaking them. My inclination would be to go with what you've got. Trust God to know what you're doing. As you said, the book could be awfully long with just the people we have—and I am amazed at how many you do have! Perhaps this is enough? I have always been thrilled to find a book wherein only one person was dialoguing. The idea of more than one is just stupendous!!

Okay, now let's see what God has to say.

Hi, God.

Hi Jo. Yes, you do go on and on. Well, at last, ready to listen?

I am not empty yet, so I will probably speak up—as the spirit will. You say not to try but to do. I do not know if I am ready to do! But here is the question:

God, here we have people who desire to have a dialog with you. Yet, they either cannot or choose not, for one reason or another. Please give some advice, practical steps, or wisdom to help these people be able/willing to converse with you.

I think they really need to know how much I love them and to feel very safe and encouraged.

Yes, in a way, they do desire. Can you help them, and are they really ready to be helped? I think they just need to be around it (dialoguing)—people doing it—to become familiar with it and at ease with it. People doing it and sharing it. I am typing this from me, though there is sort of a feeling of this also being from God here, but not clearly in words. I think people need to be able to read and share in the process. Like a child seeing its parents pray, and then feeling comfortable praying. I am hoping to develop my life into such a way that God is included in ALL my conversations—because He is always there, so why ignore Him?

Yes, I am always there and I always allow myself to be ignored—in that I do not demand you listen/hear my words. That does not mean that I do not try to get them to you.

Yes, I was amazed at the ways the others hear God. This is very exciting, because at last I am with others from whom I can learn and grow in this endeavor. Perhaps we could share at least the answers to the first question with all those who intended to participate, so they could see what is happening here, and learn, too. It would be fine with me. And, of course, God likes His words to be heard.

Yes, you are getting to know me, Jo.

I have always wanted to share dialoguing, but I am also realizing that You don't sound exactly the same to others, and it is a little discomforting. And I also feel like I am getting really confused. I thought I knew what was happening, but now there is all this disconnecting. What does it mean?

What does it mean, Jo?

That I am to spend more time directly with you. Stop being so affected by others and trying to be them—make them fit me—or make my beliefs fit theirs. That You are the way.

You have it. Come unto me. Share your me, if you like. Don't allow our relationship to be overpowered by the world even when it is so close to your path. No two paths are identical.

Thank you, and thanks to Llovit for keeping us in touch.

DJS/NB/Canada

My dear one, how do you know they desire to converse with Me? Their actions answer you. All are able to dialog; yet many are not seriously ready. The Conversations with Me through Neale Donald Walsch sparked great enthusiasm and interest in Me, however that joy of conversation gets lost in your everyday world.

There are many of you who so desperately want to believe in Me yet have not reached the stage to accept Me. You must truly believe, for dialog to be successful. Although I listen...you do not hear. I have so much more to share with you and tell you!

Cynthia Attar

Lennie/OH/USA

Ah Lennie. Give them a smile and tell them to go ahead and ask me and then listen. Listening is the important piece. Tell them not to shy away from me. Believe that they can hear me—that they are worthy of hearing me. You are all my children, all a part of me. I love each and every one of you. I am always here for you, all anyone has to do is ask.

Well, that is a very nice answer but it doesn't seem to answer Llovit's question:

> ...is there steps—a rule book, so to speak--of "How to talk to you"?

No. Anyone who desires to hear me can. The question turns in to being, "Will they listen or acknowledge me when I speak?" So smile at them. Reach their souls and let them know that they can do this.

Ok. But this is a book and people can't see my smile. How do I advise them then?

That is not your way.

Ok. But can you help me reach others through Llovit's questions for her book?

She has the answers she needs for the book on this one. You need to remember to smile. Smile in a way to reach another's soul.

Llovit/WA/USA

I figured I better go to my source within and ask for assistance on clarifying my own confusion.

Ok upstairs, there seems to be some reason people do not tap in and communicate with you through writing, like many of us have learned to do. Help me out, here. Why wouldn't they be interested into tapping into the source of their truth and answers? I don't get it.

What you are saying is easy, is not that easy for others. They disregard what you say, as it has intimidated them.

Well, I'm sorry about that. That is not my intention. But tell me, other than intimidation, why don't people write up their own god-self conversations in masses?

The world's religions are set up to take away from self-responsibility. Religions have been around for a very long time. People through the ages have not taken self-responsibility and have bowed down to the structure and control of the churches as the only way to live satisfactorily in god's eyes. You (and others) are introducing a new way, a new religion. It's called self-religion. Don't expect massive changes today from thousands of years of religious doctrine. People don't usually change that fast. You are introducing a new way, giving tools, and PLEASE allow others to shift in their own time and space.

Tell me, what kind of responsibility does self-religion bring with it?

When one is self-responsible, one knows—without a doubt—that they have created everything in their life, including their life. That means blame would be abolished, hatred would be nonexistent, and love would abound. Only those in higher evolutionary positions are prone to take this step. It is much easier and comfortable for the masses to blame and hate the source of their problems, rather than realize they are the source of their problems. The earthly shift has awakened many people. Full self-responsibility is further down the line than just becoming awakened. One awakes, looks around, sees what's going on, what works, what isn't working, begins to upgrade their life by eliminating those things that do not work anymore and somewhere down the path, one takes the step to examine self-responsibility, and consider it as truth. For you to have a publication of those who are that far along on their path that they have learned to communicate with me, is a tremendous boost to those that are awakening. You have given them something to work towards as they move on down their path. And maybe they will chose to do this work and maybe not. At some point they most likely will, as you know how valuable this skill is, and cannot live without it. Somewhat like you feel about needle nose pliers.

I do love my needle nose pliers. They are SO useful in SO many ways. Everywhere I go, I take my needle nose pliers. I have several, as I lose them all the time and go buy another pair, then the first turn up somewhere!

Yes, you have found a tool that works for you in many instances, just like your communications with me. And someday many people will find a tool that works very well for them in many instances. They may find a hammer, or a wrench, or a screwdriver, or a knife. Whatever tool they find, they can then use that tool to do many things that they couldn't without the tool, just like you have found with your communications. And just because you value your needle nose pliers, it is not necessary for you to insist that everyone else buy a pair. They will find the tool that works for them. Do you hear what I am saying?

Yes, just because communicating with you on paper works for me, doesn't mean that will be the way you will connect with others. Maybe they will find that the two of you communicate better through music or painting or something. Am I getting it?

Yes, perfectly. This method is but one method of communication. It is a clear method and can be explained better, especially in your position of desiring to write a book. Think of trying to write a book where your and my communication was in gut feelings. This would be very fine, indeed (and yes, I do communicate through this medium, also), however it would not make for the quality and clarity needed for a book. The words you get from me, written, is the method best suited for book form. Allow others to find their own method. Don't get me wrong, I love what you are doing and value every step of the way. Just know that you are presenting a meal. And if others just look at it, that is just fine. They all don't have to eat every last morsel and want to cook their own for this book to be effective. Do you understand, now?

Oh yes I do. I will just lay out my food plate for others to view if they choose, to taste what they like or put the plate aside. If they choose to cook the meal or just look at the plate, that is the perfect situation for each individual. Thank you upstairs, I DO understand now.

A separate time, I asked upstairs about logic.

Llovit/WA/USA

The difference between logical assumptions and feeling based experiences is monumental. Logic precludes experiences many times. If one is learning things through books, then that is the logic being gained. When one has the experience of what that logic is teaching, then and only then can one truly understand what the books are teaching. Now, when one experiences something, it generally is not necessary to create the logical for a complete experience. In other words, you don't have to know why, in order for it to all work as needed. Although most people prefer to work out of their logic. Just know that logic only goes so far in "truth". When discussing issues, ask for experiences. This will silence the ego, as egos generally are not focused on truth as experiences and feelings, but are focused on being right, knowing stuff, for attention and approval and gaining followers. This pertains to you, too, Llovit.

Patricia/NJ

You and Llovit have come together to develop a side of yourselves not previously recognized on the conscious level. Logic is very easy to access, as you have done that all your life. The more you know/learn, the 'better' your logic becomes. That is honorable. However, logic is so limiting. To become an unlimited being, one must push through that barrier and find a way to access the god within. To do so is the reason we all are here writing this book. It is the desire of Llovit to aid you in this process, as she is here to further the growth of many people, including you and the reader—to bridge the gap between people and their inner god. I ask of you to use the information you have available, whether in books, tapes, or other people, to begin to tap into this ultimate source—name it what you like. If you find resistance to this, please use Llovit as your target, as she will help you through your struggles. And what better way for the reader to bridge this gap than by finding folks struggling in the same manner? In other words, honesty is essential here. If you have blocks, difficulties, anger, frustrations, and even successes, write them down and email it to Llovit. She is strong, she is animal trainer, you know. Don't hold back your feelings please, as the truer your feelings, the more you will help with readers in their own struggles.

Chapter 7
The Purpose of Life

One of the most difficult questions to answer throughout the ages has been, "What is my purpose here on earth?" So many times has that question been asked, yet the asker walks away unsatisfied, only to return to this basic question again, later on. If one does find a suitable answer, it undoubtedly is not the full answer, or s/he would quit asking the question! I thought it was essential to get this information direct from upstairs and see what wisdom emerged. Therefore, this week I sent the following question on life's purpose with some instruction for the participants.

> *Question: In this question I'm looking for a down to earth answer, here! An answer I (as a simple human) can fully understand, grasp, work with, and act upon. This question is directed at you, the asker (not me, Llovit). "Why am I here on earth at this time? What is my life's purpose in this lifetime? How can I best fulfill this purpose?"*

Marilyn/Amboy/WA

You are here this lifetime to fulfill your own desires. You are here to learn about what these are and how to fulfill them. You are here to discover the meaning of life. Every single moment you are here on earth, creation is happening. It did not begin and end, but is an ever evolving process continuing on with every breath you take. You are aware of this at a cellular level. Your heart knows this is true. Your interconnected soul knows the purpose and meaning of life. Your journey is to discover this for yourself. I cannot give you the answer, for you are creating it with your life. You fulfill your purpose by being yourself, by being authentic, by becoming aware of "All That Is", in each and every moment. You often feel there is some kind of mission, some greater good, something you need to do, to help save humanity from itself.

Well that is how you used to feel, that is true. You still sometimes have these fleeting thoughts. Every single part and particle of what makes up life on earth as you know it, plays an important role. It knows what part it plays and how important and wonderful it is. When you are being authentic to yourself, when you are coming from your true self, then you do your part in helping to create a balance and a wholeness within the rest of life. It really is a personal game.

Look at all of life that surrounds you and is not human. A tree just loves being itself and in being itself, becomes a host and home to millions of other beings, from microscopic size on up to birds and squirrels and opossums and bears. It is not comparing itself to other trees and thinking it is better or less than. It is too busy being the best tree it can be. The same is true for all other parts of Nature as well. Perfection is merely being the best you, you can be.

How do you do that? How do you discover the real you? This is where the challenge lies. From the time you were born, you have been listening to others and accepting, for the most part, what they said as "the way things were." You have accepted ideas about life, love, work, food, religions, money, people, and so on, from your parents, friends, teachers, society, work, books, magazines, television ...and on and on, without question.

This is just the way life is, you told yourself. Few people actually asked you how you felt about anything. And if you had an idea which was contrary to the norm you were often ostracized. In your case, you often felt like you came from some other place, like you didn't fit in, and yet many of the beliefs you accepted were not your own. You begin to take things for granted and just expect, or assume, they happen a certain way. To be authentic requires creation come from a place of clarity. It requires courage to release every idea, thought, belief, experience you have ever had so that you can create who you really are in this moment, an authentic version of you and not all these other people. This is your challenge.

Marilyn, when you can be your authentic self, your entire life changes. When you are being the best you you can be, the world will come alive and you will see things as they truly are, not through all the layers of other people's stuff through which you often view life, clouded and confused.

Clarity brings awareness and an aliveness what is difficult to describe. Nature is alive every single moment. No two moments are ever the same. No two leaves, flowers, snowflakes, smiles, kisses, hugs, are ever the same.

When you can be fully present with each moment, savoring the richness it has to offer you, life will be filled with meaning; and the need for a purpose of some sort will fade away. Being yourself will become your fulfillment, and you will naturally be doing whatever it is that you are meant to do, here and now, in this ever present, never ending moment you call life. You will no longer take anything for granted. Each touch, each kiss, each smile, each bite of food, each nuzzle from an animal friend, will be like the first time. Your body will become alive with feelings and sensations you have not imagined, as you view a sunset, drink some water, or lay on the grass with a friend. Every person will become your lover, as you expand and understand what the Oneness of all life is about. Love is what connects all the dots and the glue the binds the universe together in harmony.

Love is something to be savored and shared equally with all of life, yourself, and every other bit of creation. Being in love with all life is being god, is being the part of god you desire to be, is becoming one with All, and part of that Oneness. So, find yourself and discover who you really are, and become the best you can be. And from that place, your life will flow forth with a richness and texture you once imagined only for gods, and for a place you once imagined existed only after death. Life is what you make it, and when you can bring it alive inside yourself, everything else will pale in comparison. Be yourself and your purpose will be fulfilled.

JofromAlaska

Hello, God.

Hi, Jo.

Here I am again, coming with a question.

Yes, you have been a little quiet this week.

Yes. God, "Why am I here on earth at this time?"

Because I want you here, my Jo. To listen.

Oh.

Yes, and to be with me.

Oh! I Know!

Yes.

"What is my life's purpose in this lifetime?"

I guess I haven't really asked You that before.

I am not sure that you have, though I always stand ready.

I guess I don't really care. Don't feel the need to ask, or the inspiration to do so. But I am asking now, for this book. To share it. I think I feel that You will tell me what You want me to know. And yet, I do seek to become what You created me to be. I just didn't think I had to ask. Thought You would tell me what I needed. Trusted You.

Trust is good. And asking can be important. I haven't inspired you to ask this question before, but someone feels it is important. (And perhaps it is inspired by me.)

Yes.

I love you, Jo. Your first purpose is to be here to experience my love. You are doing that to an extent. And you are learning to do it and to trust me and to be more aware of my love. You are enjoying and growing with Conversations with God and A Course in Miracles[3], no?

Yes, I am enjoying them both very much. I feel like my brain is being stretched and more fully used. Becoming more pure, less tainted by wrong teachings of the world. More aware of truth, and of You.

That is good. I also see that you are getting back into the Bible.

---

[3] Schucman, Helen <u>A Course In Miracles-Combined Volume</u>. Viking Press. 1996.

Yes, that is Your word for me. The first one to which I was exposed. The first one to which You exposed me.

You are beginning to see right through me, Jo. Your awareness is indeed growing in this way, and yet you are not conversing with me as much and as deeply on a strictly personal need/desire basis as at one time.

But I love You and know you are always with me.

Yes, Jo. But are you always aware of me?

No.

Correct. Your life's purpose is to become aware of me who loves you so greatly, and of others. Of what is being missed in the world, and to love where love is needed. To see and appreciate.

Is that everything? (It doesn't feel like that should be everything.)

I give you immense freedom and choice. As you learn one teaching, exercise one skill, one ability. As you solve one problem, make one headway, there will always be more. You shall not go bereft. Do the one well. That is enough. Do not worry. Do not focus on future or past too much. Be with me. That is my greatest joy, to be together in love as one.

"How can I best fulfill this purpose?"

Trust and be. As you are. Be in touch with you, with me in you, with me, with me in others, with others, with earth, with me in earth. Be.

Lennie/OH/USA

Ok, I need to get into my space. God, why am I here on this earth at this time? Ok God, I know I know the answer to this one but let's help Llovit out and have the conversation again. Let me hear your words so I can share them.

Why am I here on this earth at this time?

My dear Lennie, you are here to transform your church, to wake people up to all the love in their lives. Not just with those that they know, but every soul that they may or may not come into contact with.

This is only your beginning. I have such plans for you. I do not choose to reveal them all to you now for you will run from it. You have come so far in acknowledging the work you have to do, and you know that there is so much more to it. Haven't you wondered what it is going to look like? No, you haven't. For you right now, it is just enough to know that there is more.

How can I best fulfill this purpose?

Listen, listen, listen and then get into action. Trust in me to provide you with the support that you need. I'm not going to leave you alone to accomplish your work. If you are aware, you will see the people who can help you. Don't be attached to who they may be, they could be all and everyone. Just keep listening.

It is interesting that you are skipping Llovit's second question, "What is my life's purpose in this lifetime?" You have a hint that it is bigger than you, and it is. Don't be afraid, you will not be left alone. Trust in me. All there is, is love. Remember that and remember that I do love you completely.

LittleSoul/Anadarko/OK

Right now LittleSoul you are on earth to do absolutely nothing but to experience relativity. Every purpose possible is your life's purpose because life never ends and life never begins. Life is a cycle. And in this cycle you have had every present purpose.

Well, what about this present consciousness/body I contain? What is its purpose?

You do not have a body life purpose. You have present purposes, which I have not set for you, but you have set for you. These purposes you know; for they are to teach people to be more loving and evolved. Being evolved and loving yourself, and many more. Of course these purposes can change at any time, and will. You could move from teaching people to be loving, to being so enlightened you can heal people (one "miracle") to doing many "miracles" at a time, as a master would. You are in tune with your soul much more than before, so you are conscious of your soul's main goal, which is to experience complete love, happiness, and power, with the absence of fear—which is mastery.

But those present purposes you stated, I am already doing.

Yes, you have chosen to stay at this level of love for the time being. When you decide to move on, or back (whatever you desire), you will decide that, not me.

Yeah, I am happy staying right here at this level, but I doubt I'll move back...

That's what you choose now, and you also choose to stay at this level now. Maybe sometime in the future you'll create different things for yourself, onward or backward. And whatever you choose is because that is what your soul is ready for, and that is wonderfully perfect, my divine child.

SAM/Clinton/Mass

Lately God, I feel like I've been leaving you out. I've gotten distracted the past week or so, and I'm sorry.

No need to be sorry.

I know ...and thank you for that.

What have you noticed since you have gotten distracted?

That I've gone back to some of my old ways of being stressed out and conscious of what people were thinking of me. Insecure, I guess. I just keep telling myself ...none of this matters ...it's all my own reality ...there is no end. It helps most of the time, if I think about it all day in everything I do. But when I get distracted it's hard to make that crossover back into the love and peace of your arms. I don't know why it would be so difficult. You would think it would be easy because it's definitely the more pleasant of the two. You would think people would be drawn to want to create the best of who they are. But sometimes ...even when you begin to remember ...it's a struggle.

Why am I here on earth at this time?

You chose to be.

Am I evolving?

Constantly! Can't you feel it? You are understanding and that is the battle that everyone else is fighting!

But I don't feel like I always practice what I understand. I've slipped up in the past week.

But see it for what it is. You are seeing the creation of your stress. You are gathering proof that when you forget the basic simple truths that it does not serve you. You worry needlessly and unproductively. But you see it for what it is and that is a huge step.

Step to where?

To where you want to be.

And where's that?

You tell me...

I want to be able to travel with my husband and remain as happy as we are today for the rest of our lives. I want to be able to help my family and friends including those I do not know. I want to help give everyone a chance for opportunity. I want to experience success in all areas of my life.

Take out the want and you will get there faster. Act as if you already have these things and you will make your reality sooner than later.

So, is my life's purpose to accomplish these things?

If you choose.

My life's purpose is to choose? Isn't it to remember who I am?

If that is your choice. Many people have lived their entire lives without a distinct understanding that they have remembered "who they are". Many people leave their bodies very satisfied with their experience of that life ...even if they don't "remember". Their choice is their path.

But wouldn't they have had a more peaceful and less stressful life had they remembered?

It depends on what they expected from life ...whether or not they were disappointed. Are you disappointed?

I used to be ...before I chose to acknowledge that you are a huge part of my life.

Why is that?

Because I always felt like I was fighting the current ...alone. When I was a child, I felt special ...like I was going to accomplish something special. And then when I grew older I forgot I was special, and focused on fitting in with the rest of the world—or at least fitting in with my world around me.

That is a good distinction. The rest of the world versus the "world around me". Do you know why?

Because the world around me is my own perspective.

Exactly! Not everyone is the same. You felt you were special when you were young and you made a conscious choice to do special things. When you were older you remembered what you once wanted to do, yet you looked around you and you saw nothing happening the way you expected it to be ...So you felt even more lost trying to fit into a world that you originally never saw. When you were a child you did whatever felt right for you.

Yes, and life was fun, and then it became difficult.

That is simply because you weren't following your path. You got lost but I see now that you have experienced what you don't want out of life and you can look at it and see it for what it is. Just an experience ...that can be changed.

Thank you ...that is so freeing. Okay, so how is the best way to fulfill what I want to fulfill?

Know what it is that you want fulfilled. Be clear on exactly what you want to do right now. Be clear on how what you are doing right now is getting you to where you want to be.

It seems simple ...almost too simple.

It is simple ...perfectly simple. Not to say that you won't come across obstacles ...but know that they are there to guide you ...See them for what they are and know that whatever you chose to do today can be changed tomorrow ...if you chose it to. Remember ...nothing is right or wrong ...it serves you or it doesn't. Make that distinction. Keep your perspective focused on what you now remember ...You ARE special ...You DO special things ...YOU ARE creating who you are ...Remember that now is the time to be and to become ...Don't focus so much on the "planning to be". BE right now. Do you understand?

Yes I do, but what if I'm being and not doing.

If you are being who you want to be, then you will do what reflects that. At first you need to be very aware of your actions ...How are they reflecting who you want to be? Conscious thought. You have been doing things your whole life without it ...it will take some effort to change what you do or think by habit ...but that is perfect. You wanted to be special when you were a child, and then you experienced the feeling of not being special. You experienced having no fear as a child and then you experienced having fear as a teenager and adult. Which serves you best?

Having no fear ...it was freeing and fun ...everything seemed attainable.

It is.

So basically ...I am what I am ...not what I will be ...for I will never be that which will be.

Yes! Saying I "will" or I "want" is not as productive as saying I "am". Create your reality ...don't wait for it to happen because in reality you are ALWAYS creating your reality...

Thank you God for helping me to understand that. I love you!

Tiaka/Japan

I am here at this time to remember who I am, which is god being in the body. To love all of my inner and outer selves unconditionally and reunite my physical, emotional, logical, mental, spiritual, light, infinite, finite bodies as one here on earth. This is available to everyone at this time, if they choose. It is an unprecedented opportunity to release the limitations and restrictions we have purposely held over ourselves since the downfall of Atlantis.

To know that it is all perfect and to see through the marvelous illusion. I am god being in the body, being in the universe made of the larger source of god (the rest of me/you/everything). To unite all that was perceived as evil and good as one within me.

The second coming is really a first global coming. The universe is now witness to the first birth of a fully realized god conscious being in the body on a planetary scale. We are a model for the universe, as this is the source's desire for all life forms to remember their true nature. Of course, this has not been an easy ride. Yet our fall into density and separation has provided a unique path to source consciousness while still in the body. The light and darkness is now uniting within us to form a new being. A fully enlightened one that can love all unconditionally and bring the universe to the next stage of creation.

Free will is manifest in all creation. However, this opportunity will be available, only if you wish or choose it. If you are not ready or willing to accept your evolution, then that is perfect too. You may continue the life you lead forever, if you desire.

The level of energy now entering the planet and your bodies, direct from the source (indeed you are the source being in the body) is reaching ever stronger and powerful levels. Information is now available, that was once kept secret. This was to allow us to grow within confinement and limits. Yes, it has seemed at times a dark and difficult route, yet believe me when I say your soul cries out with unending joy at our self fulfillment of our conscious enlightenment.

What's next, you ask? Humanity will once more become a galactic society and bring free-willed, unconditionally loving, biological creation to all parts of the universe. It is indeed a journey to the stars. There will be those who wish to stay on earth and that is fine, too. But when you are fully aware of your potential, you may wish to join your brothers and sisters on faraway planets. We have struggled for naught. There is a divine blueprint, yet with our free will, only we can choose to fulfill our destiny. Yet once you remember you are god being in the body and what is manifest on the outside is you also, as god being the universe, all can be united as one source being itself.

Perfection. Wow!

Your inner flame is now brightening from that of a candle flame to a super nova!! That is how wonderful a time it is at present. We are all blessed to be able to fulfill our collective dreams! Thanks and love to you all. Mother earth is also raising her vibration and will take her body to new levels of expression. Colors, sights, sounds, animals, plants, etc., will look as never before. Heaven on earth, heaven from earth.

Simply, you are an angel in physicality and have now awoken to your potential. This is unlimited. It is now your turn to create!

Norma/Mexico

Hi Llovit, it took a little while, but I got the answer. I've been kind of blue these days, so I've been postponing this conversation with God. Finally I ask him today:

"Dear Father, Can you tell me what is the mission I have NOW, in this life? Dear Father, what do you want me to do?"

Do nothing for me. Whatever you do, do it for you. Love for you, care for you, learn for you. Whatever disguises the reminder has, you'll recognize it in the right moment for you to do so. So don't be afraid nor sad, [be]cause I'm your loving Father, and I won't leave you alone.

There you have it!! I don't know if this answer works for your book, it certainly worked for me.

The following is a compilation of a few subjects that include and address the purpose of life.

Patricia/NJ

God, what do many people ask you? Like what is your most common question people want answers to?

The why of life, life's purpose for them.

And...

How to be happy. Actually, people think they know how to have permanent happiness. But when it's only temporary, they ask again. I'm talking about material things and outside things such as getting a specific job, making a specific someone like them, etc. These people really want permanent happiness, yet they won't listen to my answers and communications, as it's not what they want to hear. The quick fix is only temporary. So much energy is expended on temporary happiness.

Just remember, you are in control and create your life. You have set all these human beings around you into motion at your command, even the ones you don't think you want there, have strategically been placed by you, for a learning, as a mirror, or simply to experience something.

Llovit/WA/USA

When a person is born in today's society, that soul knows the complete picture of what he wants to accomplish in this lifetime and sets up the circumstances to his liking that will enable him to do what he wants. Shortly before birth, the veil of forgetfulness is draped and the soul and the child are somewhat separate. There is a part of the child which knows the soul picture, but cannot express it, as it is too young. During the course of living, the child is hugely influenced by his environment, parents and others. The veil becomes thick as a blanket and all recollection of past lives or the meaning of this lifetime falls away under the spell of forgetfulness. In that, the child forgets that he is part of All That Is. The child forgets that he houses god in his soul. The child takes on the thoughts of the parents—the forgetfulness of the parents. Through the years, the child becomes more and more separate. As a young adult, the desire to connect grows stronger, especially if the child moves out on his own. This is usually when most people realize how separate they are and want to rectify it.

Can you help me with "the big picture"? Like the big picture of life, religion, etc.

What is your ultimate goal?

To be one with you.

Why?

Cause then I will be in Love, peace, joy.

So, the goal is Love, peace and joy?

Yes, and oneness.

Ok, I will buy that. Are you now in Love, peace, joy?

More and more as I learn and grow and evolve. It is where I want to be as much as possible and still learn, grow and evolve.

Do you think others want this, too?

Yes. I believe this is the goal of most all people.

I won't chastise you for your belief that you are the same as everyone else. Just widen your mind a bit. All have very different paths to walk, in very different ways. Some may not be anywhere near Love, peace, joy and therefore do not have those goals. They have "lesser" goals that eventually may lead to Love, peace, joy; but at this moment, everyone is in a different space than you and have different wants/desires/needs.

Ok, ok, I stand corrected. Let's get back to the big picture. If people want different things, how can there be a big picture?

Each individual chooses how s/he lives his life with his individual goals. S/he does this through a combination of upbringing, morals, desire for better, growth, beliefs and love. Each individual does/acts in accordance to all these things and strives to keep inner peace. Some have peace as ultimate goal, some have love as ultimate goal. Some have joy, some connection, some freedom, some happiness. When person "A" behaves in a certain manner, usually it is to restore inner peace. Inner peace seems to be the focus of many, rather than joy or Love or the others. When inner peace is disturbed, the human sets off to rebalance itself. It does this through a variety of means, usually attributed to beliefs.

Joe believes beating someone up will restore his peace, so that is what he does. Is he wrong? Is he bad? Is he off track? He is doing what he thinks will restore peace and balance within him. He may feel some satisfaction upon the beating (if he 'wins'). And this lasts for a short while. In his mind, he succeeded. In the long run, he created another imbalance, due to [the] belief that he did something wrong. However, that imbalance will not surface immediately and the satisfaction [of fighting] does surface immediately. Therefore, the short sided Joe concludes that beatings restore his balance and inner peace, never seeing that beatings actually take him further away from that inner peace he desires. Now Joe has guilt, disarray, yucky feelings to contend with. Yet the more subtle of these feelings are more distantly connected. In other words, the latter set of feelings are not apparent to him nearly as much as a result of beatings. Short sighted Joe feels beatings equal satisfaction and disregards the beatings actually creating dissatisfaction, which come up after the temporary satisfaction. The term for today's world is immediate gratification. Joe connects beatings with immediate gratification, ignoring the long term effects.

You are very good. Thank you. I'm really tired. I got to go now.

Chapter 8
When to Help and When to Allow?

A man found a cocoon of a butterfly. One day a small opening appeared in the cocoon. He sat and watched the emerging butterfly for several hours as it struggled to force its body through that tiny hole to get out. Then, it seemed to stop making any progress. It appeared as if the butterfly had gotten as far as it could and could go no further. Then the man decided to help the butterfly, so he took a pair of scissors and snipped off the remaining bit of the cocoon.

The butterfly then emerged easily, but it had a swollen body and small, shriveled wings. The man continued to watch the butterfly because he expected that, at any moment, the wings would enlarge and expand to be able to support the body, which would contract in time. Neither happened! In fact, the butterfly spent the rest of its life crawling around with a swollen body and shriveled wings. It never was able to fly.

What the man in his kindness and haste did not understand, was that the restricting cocoon and the struggle required for the butterfly to get through the tiny opening was God's way of forcing fluid from the body of the butterfly into its wings so that it would be ready for flight once it achieved its freedom from the cocoon.

Sometimes struggles are exactly what we need in our life. If we went through our life without any obstacles, it would cripple us. We would not be as strong as what we could have been. And we could never fly.

Ok upstairs, this is my question for the week.

> *"When do we help others and when do we allow them to struggle out of their own cocoon?"*

SAM/Clinton/Mass

I had a hard time with this question because it relates so closely with a question that I, too, have been trying to answer.

Since I have become more interested in my own spirituality and since I have opened myself up to God and have become a better listener and a more conscious thinker, ...my life has literally transformed and I see how so many are burdened by needless worry and so on. I feel the need to help these people out ...especially those so close to me. I've found resistance to my new-found beliefs and have not been sure how I should continue to get my point across.

For example ...My husband and I are starting our own business ...yet he is still working full time. He worries endlessly about money ...having it ...losing ...never getting enough ...etc. We are no doubt taking some big risks with our small savings ...yet I remain...neutral. I trust in God and I feel that we are being led to success and I am prepared to hit some bumps along the way. My husband is an "all or nothing" type person and I fear if we are not successful right away ...he will sink into depression and call the whole thing a waste of time and money. He says things like ... "I'll be happy when we have at least $x [a specific amount of money] in the bank..." or "I'll stop worrying so much once I see some progress..." ...stuff like that. I try to convince him that we create what we think ...so be happy now ...pretend we are already successful and that it is just a matter of time that we will see it created before us. He is under the impression that worrying is a safeguard against jumping too quickly. It is very frustrating to see him stress out so much, needlessly. So what can I do to speed up the process of his understanding?

Be an example.

But that just doesn't seem like enough.

You cannot teach a student until the student is ready to learn ...and even then ...it is not a learning process but a process of understanding.

What do I do when he asks me for help? When he says he's stressed out and needs comforting.

Comfort him and love him and then look to understand what he is really asking.

What do you mean by that?

Understand the problem. As in the case of the butterfly. The man thought he knew the problem of the butterfly ...he tried to fix a problem that he didn't understand. He made things worse. First ...wait to be asked. Had the man waited to be asked by the butterfly, he would not of made the problem that didn't exist in the first place worse.

A butterfly can't ask for help. What if I come upon a person who is knocked unconscious and can't ask ...I should not help him?

The way to help that person would be to understand the problem...would you know why this person is unconscious? ...If you did ...would you know how to fix the problem? You would most likely call or get help ...help that you don't know how to give yourself. If that man called someone who knew a thing about butterflies ...he would have known that he should not interfere. You know more about people than about butterflies so you would no doubt observe that this man needs help ...but you would also realize that unless you were a doctor ...you would not be able to determine the problem.

But I just feel that if my husband read the CWG 1,2,3 books that he would come to remember so much faster.

Indeed ...and he has access to them?

Yes ...to that and more. ...I have many books that have helped me.

Did someone give you those books or did you ask someone for those books?

No ...it was a process that has taken about a year or two to come to these books.

Do you think if someone handed you the books five years ago ...things would be different?

Maybe ...but now that you mention it, someone did give me a similar book of the ones I read now. And I was just thinking yesterday that I wish I could remember the title because I gave it back and never read it.

Why didn't you read it?

I was into reading fiction ...at the time ...not spirituality...actually I thought from the title that it was going to be too "out there" for me to actually believe.

But it's not now.

No.

Why?

Because I guess ...I had to go through "the process" I went through. I'm beginning to understand what you're getting at. My husband needs to go through his own process of remember "who he is". Is that what you're saying?

Everyone has their own path and it is a path of understanding ...not of learning. You cannot teach this stuff ...it can only be explained...and it is explained most effectively when one asks for it to be explained. There are different levels of understanding ...one cannot skip from being constant "worry wart" to a master of spirituality ...just as one cannot be taught to be a master. He has come a long way ...as you have too, wouldn't you say?

Yes ...two years ago ...he said that he was fine with the fact that he was going to have to work a job that he didn't enjoy until he retired ...He said it was just the way things were and that that was reality. He thought I was a dreamer and that scared him.

Why did that scare him?

Because, we have been connected for centuries? Because they are, have been, and will be, teachers, reminders, and schoolmates? I think because he felt responsible to make me happy and he was afraid I wanted more than he could give.

What was the problem ...do you see it?

The problem is ...was ...he was under the impression that he had to make me happy in some way and that he was limited. Also he links happiness with money.

So ...the problem centered around you and your happiness?

Well no ...he wasn't happy either ...but he resigned himself to believe that no one was happy except a special few ...and they were lucky.

So the problem was that he wasn't happy?

Yes ...that and that he associates being happy with money.

Why do you think he's "come a long way"?

He's more open to risk ...we're doing something he never would have conceived of doing.

How did he get from there to here?

I took a leave of absence from my job without telling him I was going to...to write my novel ...then I got laid off ...he thought our world was crumbling and I felt that it was all my fault. I started the business on my own. He got involved after he had an inspiration of an idea. After that he got excited and that is where we are now.

Do you see what you did? You became ...selfish ...You decided to make yourself happy. You could have found another job to make him happy which would ultimately give you both his reality and you would both be unhappy. You did it for yourself and he observed. He came to an understanding that the sky would not fall if you followed your own dream.

Yes, but now he's more miserable than ever with his job because now he wants to follow his dreams yet feels stuck in his job.

Keep following your dreams. Comfort him ...love him ...do not judge him...do not teach him. Act as I act toward you. When you ask ...I answer...but I leave it up to you to listen and act. I am not frustrated when it takes you awhile to get it ...The problem you are feeling lies with you ...not him.

Really?

Yes. You were once very frustrated that he was not a dreamer like yourself and that scared you. You too had doubts that his "realistic views" would not make you happy. On your path you discovered that YOU make YOU happy...no one else can make YOU happy when you are less than happy about yourself.

You're right! I had feelings that I had big dreams and he, my new husband, would hold me back. That was scary. I even questioned if maybe we weren't supposed to be together even though I love him so much.

So what did you do?

I prayed to you all the time to show me my way ...to show me how to get to where I wanted to go. I listened for you and you answered me. Ultimately I stopped using my husband as an excuse and took responsibility for my own happiness, and things got tremendously better. It was all an amazing experience of discovery.

You want him to be on the same level you are at without going through his own amazing experience?

Not exactly ...when you put it like that. But ...it seems things would be easier if we were experiencing this all together.

No doubt ...but you must be patient ...observe ...understand...love ...he is on a path ...he just doesn't know exactly where he wants to be yet. It will come when he is ready.

But I thought we were supposed to be the source ...spread the word.

Be the source, yes! Spread understanding ...Spread love ...Neale Donald Walsch wrote books yet he forces no one to read them ...but millions have.

I understand ...but it is still going to be difficult, I think.

Every parent goes through the same dilemma yet the more successful parents are the ones who set the best examples and allow their children to find their own path.

Thank you God ...this has been bugging me for quite awhile.

You were open to listen today ...you haven't been in awhile.

You're right. Thank you for being there when I was ready.

I'm here even when you're not ready.

I love you.

Thank you and I love you.

Marilyn/Amboy/WA

When do I offer help and when do I not?

Marilyn, offering help, as you saw in this example, is not always in the best interest of those concerned. Sometimes, for instance, people offer free food or housing or clothing and people become more and more dependent on that support and much less self sufficient. You see two people fighting and you sometimes want to break it up, assuming this would be in their best interest; and someone gets seriously hurt or killed partly because you became involved.

Even with something as simple as teaching. You did an awesome job sometimes, raising your children. Awesome, because it was so difficult for you. You learned from Madame Montessori[4] it is best to offer assistance to a child, only when they ask for it. You would watch your son or daughter struggling to learn to tie their shoe, or draw, or button a shirt, and had tremendous patience. What you had learned was, in interrupting them and saying "Here let me show you how to do that." you are saying to the child that they are a failure in that moment and need some assistance. In waiting for them to come to you instead, you allowed them to develop the self confidence necessary to ask for help only when they are unable to achieve their goal on their own. Only they could tell, when they had tried all the alternatives they were aware of. This inspired their creativity and their willingness to keep going under difficult circumstances later on in life. The other technique encourages children to give up easily and to feel they cannot do much on their own, without help from someone else. Sadly, most parents lose patience quickly and so a life long lesson is lost. A good rule of thumb is to offer help when you are asked to do so. Offer

---

[4] A specialized children's school (http://www.montessori.org/)

help in a way which inspires those involved to create or discover their own solutions. Do not assume to "know better".

How about war?

In war, you always, always have people who have agreed to participate. There is no one who forces someone to take a gun in their hand and kill. Killing is always unnecessary. You have heard of case after case where someone remained in a space of love, and the person who was threatening them, backed off and left. You (industrialized societies) still work on the mentality that the bigger the guns and missiles, the more powerful the country. Nothing could be further from the truth. You do not maintain peace, create peace, teach peace, inspire peace, by the use of any kind of weapon which creates fear or kills another being. Wars create death on many more levels than merely the human one, which you choose to recognize. Only when you look deeper, will you realize peace is created from within. And from that space of pure love, you CAN make a difference and you CAN help in many ways you have not even begun to imagine.

By imagining the butterfly in all its beauty, you provide an assistance that is beyond measure and which inspires the butterfly to be all it can be. By imagining peace, you help create it. If all the people in your country prayed for peace, it would do far more to provide assistance than all the guns and bombs and military you could imagine. Come always from a place of love and you will no longer need to question your actions. You will know, always, what to do.

Tiaka/Japan

Help is given when sought or when you feel it is needed. There are many instances when help is actually forced change in the guise of help, such as country-directed bombings. This may work, yet at what cost to lives, the environment, and thought to future acts of revenge? If war is seen to help peace, then why didn't the wars of the Romans end violence within Europe? There will be people whose consciousness will change as a result of war. And there will also be those, as a result, will harbor malice and hatred for the opposing side. In any situation where you feel help is needed, try to remember how would unconditional love act?

Forced change through war is given in the hope of instilling peace, therefore peace is expected and is as such, a condition. Unconditional love and giving of time, aid, food, blankets, peace negotiations, advisors, expects nothing and no outcomes in return. It is condition-less. Homeless people need food, shelter, and warmth. They also need love in abundance. They need help in reorganizing their life. Only! Only if it is what they seek. Trying to force a homeless person off the street may work for a short period, yet change (everlasting) comes about from inner self, not from the outside. We can advise and help in any situation and expect nothing in return. When and how to give help? When you think of when and how you would accept help. Remember, the world is perfect. Nothing needs to be changed, unless it was what you and the other desire and search for. God, the source, knows this is an illusion and we are experiencing pain, loss, forgetfulness and fear in order to re-member by our own free will and choice that we are indeed god being in the body! We decide our evolution. When we want to change, that is perfect also.

JofromAlaska

Hi, God. Here I am with another question. And, by the way, thank you for this gloriously beautiful spring day!

You are more than welcome, Jo. Every one is, though not everyone is enjoying it as much as you are. (Yes, and some are enjoying it even more!) My delight is in seeing my gifts appreciated, enjoyed, noticed. It is especially nice when someone bothers to thank me. So, I thank you for your thanks. Got another question, huh? Llovit keeps coming up with them doesn't she?

Yes she does, and good ones!

Thank you.

You are welcome.

So, for the listening audience, would you care to reiterate on this one?

You bet. It is,

"When do we help others and when do we allow them to struggle out of their own cocoon?"

Yup, great question, if I do say so myself.

Yes, it is one I have spent much time thinking about, even though it is one that I have not asked you. And I know it is one that I do not think about or take into consideration enough.

Well, you certainly all could do it more. But of course you love so much to 'play God' and solve things yourselves. You love to rescue people, to be the 'hero'. You like to see things solved, so that you aren't required to see them and suffer through them in empathy with others that I have given them to, or allowed to, receive them for their needs.

But how do we know when a problem is THEIR lesson to solve, and when it has come to us as OUR lesson to solve?

Ah, you are asking me!

Yes, that is what I am doing.

And that is what you must do, ask me.

That's it?

Isn't that enough?

LittleSoul/Anadarko/OK

You help others when you feel it's the right time. You allow them to struggle on their own when you feel so. If you choose to go a different way, you may allow them to tell you when they are ready for help and when they want to learn on their own. Let's say you have a seventeen year old who is very open to you because you are such a wise parent, [and who] desires to go have beer at a party. You would tell him all that you possibly can find on beer and let him make his own decision. You would also tell him your personal preference in what he does, but you are not trying to control him. Ask him to give you the address to where this party is, and tell him you will be home to call if he does choose to drink (you will also tell him the consequences of drinking and driving).

Now, he is at this party, drunk. He asks a friend to call you to come and pick him up. You do, and he goes to bed and has a rather painful hangover in the morning. But he is safe because he asked you for help ...But what if the story went a different way? Maybe your son is too drunk to realize the un-safety (which you told him), and decides to drive home. He gets in a wreck on the way. It is not severe, for he will fully heal, but he has to undergo 6 months of physical therapy, which can be painful. In this, he has learned on his own, and knows from experience not to do it again; although he knows from your telling him that his injuries could have been much worse. This is a choice that is up to you. You can become a controlling parent at a time like this if you feel it is your truth, or you can give him all the proper information and let him make his own decisions. Either way, you will be as wise as you are, so shall it be. Either way, it will turn out alright. If "death" occurs in this situation, he will have another life if he chooses. Not only that, but between these bodily lives he will be completely engulfed in love, and he will go to the next life a wiser being, unless he chooses not to.

Lennie/OH/USA

Ok god, this is my question for the week.

> *"When do we help others and when do we allow them to struggle out of their own cocoon?"*

Follow me on this one. Listen for me to direct you. You will know what is right for you to do the right response. To give another trust in me, trust in yourself. Follow the rhythm you will hear.

Well, that doesn't seem to be a direct answer.

It doesn't? Well of course it cannot be, each person is an individual, each soul has a different path to follow. Some would not like the intrusion. There is no pat answer, so listen. Listening really is the key. The answers are there. I will provide an opening. You have got to trust in me and listen.

Ok, well how about a person who doesn't know how to listen to god for direction—how do they help someone?

Mistakes are then made, damage is done. Remember each soul came here to heal or experience something. Do not rob them of that chance. Give compassion, yes. Do what you hear me tell you; what your highest thought directs you to. Do but do not rob them.

Chapter 9
Where Does Money Fit into Our Lives?

The age-old concern about money is frequently on most people's mind. This question is to bring clarity to this concern.

> *Question: "Upstairs, where does money fit into our lives? Everyone needs money, as nobody wants to live poorly, always struggling. However, greediness is not the answer either. So, God, where is the balance when it comes to money?"*

Tiaka/Japan

Money, money, money. It is just a form of energy we project our fears, joys, lusts, emotions, creations onto. Money, as such, is neither good nor bad—it just is. Have you ever seen what happens to money that goes out of circulation? It is burnt in a large furnace and changes form again.

As such, energy can be used for any purpose you see fit. When you feel you don't have enough money, this is really a physical manifestation of something you feel is lacking in yourself. Perhaps a lack of respect, confidence, responsibility, pride, worthiness—the list is endless. The amount of money you have will tell you what you are thinking about yourself inside.

Would you like to have more money? Then first, perhaps you should search for what your spirit is lacking. Why is it that rich people who have the means to buy anything, never seem satisfied? They are always wanting more. Is this what you desire? Is a wealth of material possessions what you really want? Then perhaps it is because you feel there is a lack of self love. To fill the gap, you surround yourself with material wealth. However, the gap will only widen and you will be disappointed with your things and thus seek to buy bigger, faster, glitzier items. And when you lose those things to fire or accident or theft, you weep at the loss. Yet you truly weep at the inability of yourself to find true happiness within.

There is nothing wrong with having money. But think to yourself and ask why you need so much money? What is your purpose? If it is for safety or security, you could find nature and/or thieves taking your safety away in a second. Feeling sure of yourself will provide an everlasting feeling of safety. Again we find that money is merely a tool of creation to experience who you believe yourself to be at any given time. Enjoy the money for what it is. Yet if it is true eternal spiritual happiness you are searching for, this will be found within your heart. In the meantime, enjoy creating with your money and try not to worry. Remember that no matter how much money you have, you will never be truly satisfied; as your vision of yourself will expand to spend that money. There is more than enough money. Just ask yourself what you wish to create with it, and if those creations are helping you discover yourself. Have fun.

Lennie/OH/USA

Just wanted to let you know I did receive the question on money. The answer isn't ready to be typed yet.

Oh it isn't.

Well, I didn't think so. Besides I'm tired.

Too tired to talk with God?

Well, kind of. I'll feel guilty if I said yes.

Might only take a minute to answer her question then you won't have to worry about it.

All right. Let's give it a round and see where it goes. ...so where is the balance?

There is no balance.

Ok, how does money fit into our lives?

Any way you want.

Profound Writings from Everyday People

I thought I wasn't supposed to 'want' anything.

Ok, you got me there. Money will show up any way you desire it. You have been wanting it.

I have? I thought that I've had a pretty good sponsoring thought about money. And that it is getting even more pronounced.

Yeah, you've done ok with it. You haven't always kept the 'sentence' the same, though. Keep choosing the same thing day in-day out. And yes, you do attract money.

Thank you. I'm trying.

Don't try, do.

There's that Yoda thing again.

Yup.

Ok, I'm too tired for this. Can we try it tomorrow?

Sure thing.

JofromAlaska

Hi, God. Thank you for this beautiful glorious sunny day, with the fresh snow on the ground, a winter wonderland once again.

Yes, thank you for appreciating it, Jo. It is lovely, isn't it?

It certainly is. It is nice to experience it—sort of meditate in it. So different from the question I am avoiding here. Okay, the question is:

"*God, where does money fit into our lives?*"

Hum ...Money. "Root of all evil", I have heard it said.

Yes, that is an expression. Is it true?

Hum ...Money is recompense— substitute.

And it is power—or can obtain power?

Yes, money can obtain power—if you allow it.

How do you NOT allow it?

Don't allow it.

Like in government—the candidates need money to campaign to get elected, and the ones that give them the money then have influence on them. Especially, I would imagine, if the candidate wants other big contributors to contribute, it has to be worthwhile to the contributor. This is all very confusing to me. What to do about this? How to get people to be altruistic? How to get myself to be altruistic? My heart is just not into this money question.

Yes, you have been busy online and with my Course in Miracles[5].

Yes, it looks/sounds quite interesting. Which book should I get?

Don't sweat the small stuff, Jo. I think you can decide that one for yourself. You just really aren't in the mood for listening to me tonight, are you?

Well, not about money —I really am not very interested in it.

Fine with me.

LittleSoul/Anadarko/OK

Money can fit into your life in any way you choose. The problem is that too many people choose not to have it (unconsciously), and are in denial about that. They can also choose to have it in the form in which they are not ready to have it. Maybe they need money to come in a different form for them to be happy with it.

If you know you have enough and give some away just for fun, it can give you a wonderful feeling about it. You will feel happier with yourself and people will credit you for it.

No one needs money. Needing something can keep that thing away from you. If you are in need, you are merely desiring with stress added. Take out the stress and you will get what you desire with no worries. Your mind also won't be clogged up with negativity, so you will be able to use your money more wisely.

---

[5] Schucman, Helen <u>A Course In Miracles-Combined Volume</u>. Viking Press. 1996.

Greed is also another form of desire, with some negativity added to it. Greed is desire with obsession mixed in it. If you get too caught up in getting money, you miss getting it. And you also miss out on how it can make you happy (which is by using it wisely). Greed also clogs your mind to use it unwisely.

Marilyn/Amboy/WA

Money never has been, or will be, an issue in people's lives, where I am concerned. I did not create money, myself. Money is a creation of human beings, and as such, has taken on an entire meaning and value of its own. It is viewed around the globe in varying degrees; from a means of barter or exchange all the way up to how you value or separate one human being from another. There is little clarity or agreement on this issue as far as I can tell. I do not create people suffering, struggling, being in need. All those things are created by people themselves.

You desire to learn things, to become more "godlike" perhaps in some ways. And so you make choices every single moment of your life. You come into this incarnation, and others, with ideas and goals and constantly change these as you go along. Money is purely what you make of it. You create money as your life with your beliefs. You value it as such and bring it to yourself or separate yourself from it by these means. You cannot hate people who have lots of money and then also desire yourself to have lots of money, because then you would feel people would hate you, too. Is this not so?

You see people struggle to make ends meet. Is that their choice? Are they teaching you to take responsibility for helping others? Do they create feelings of guilt? Some people who appear to be struggling are in reality very happy. In fact, some of them would not desire the responsibility of a whole bunch of material possessions. Human beings created money like they create pollution, like they create traffic jams. I allow you the gift to create your own lives. Do not ask me why I allow people to struggle, because I do not. Life is a choice and you make it with your own thoughts and beliefs.

If you want more money in your life, then create it. Believe and act as if you were wealthy. See yourself having and doing things you would like to do. Like a child, use your imagination and see it becoming reality now. Remember, you get what you focus on. If you focus on what you don't have, then that is where you will remain. If you focus on what you have and all the blessing and wealth you already possess, then you can, from this place, create more and more. Think about it. You are very creative and the possibilities are endless and limitless, only you can put on the breaks and stop the flow. Only you ...not me. Love, God

SAM/Clinton/Mass

Money fits into our lives in whatever way we choose. Some choose to be controlled by money. In this ...I mean they base their degree of happiness or unhappiness on how much they have, versus how much they desire to have. When this is the case ...these people are plagued by worry ...stress ...and ultimately UN-happiness for they think that in order to be happy...stress-free and worry-free they must obtain some variable amount of money.

The problem is this: 1, The variable is forever changing ...whatever they obtain they feel they need more ...they get more and somehow still feel unhappy and stressed out ...so maybe if I have more ...it will cure me. 2, Whatever is in the bank is not only never enough ...what if something happens and it is lost ...more worry ...more stress.

Some choose to not associate happiness with money thus alleviating unnecessary stress. Money is not evil just as it is not "heavenly" ...It is created by man ...as is all the stress that surrounds it.

If you are doing something "just for the money" that is your choice but it might not bring you the happiness and stress-free life your soul desires. When you are doing something for the pure pleasure of it and money happens to be the by-product of it ...you will find that money will come to you much easier than you might think.

Desire everything ...need nothing. When you need something ...expectations of why it is needed attaches itself to the "need". Whenever there are expectations ...disappointment assuredly follows. Desire money if you choose. Money can be a wonderful part of your life but it would not serve you best to make it all of your life.

But what about our basic needs?

Basic needs should be a given. It would serve you best if this was the case. If, in fact, it were the case ...you would clearly see that money is not a necessity for a happy life. But since this is not the case in your world, I can see how stressful it could be to have to depend on green pieces of paper just to break even.

However ...as I said, do what makes your soul happy ...find that happiness first, even if you have to rearrange a few things to make it possible ...find happiness first. Also give to others what you desire for yourself then you are thus giving to yourself. This may pertain to this project. What is it that you desire in making contributions to this book? Is it a desire to sharpen your god-skills? ...Is it a desire to help others who later read the book?. ...Is it a desire to project a sponsoring thought out to the world? Is it to make a lot of money? Neither answer is right or wrong but it would serve you best to have a conscious thought about why you are contributing.

SAM/Clinton/Mass

Hi Llovit ...I am writing you again regarding the money issue. I must tell you that I still find it hard not to feel uncomfortable about desiring money.

What makes you so uncomfortable.

I associate money with greed and when I acknowledge my desire for it ...I feel greedy. I'm awaiting an answer. ...I'm stuck ...this is how I've felt since I sent you the last email.

Why do you desire money?

I desire to travel the world ...I desire my husband and I to be able to spend every minute together doing whatever we want to do ...I desire that he (my husband) not be so stressed out all the time worrying about money.

Do you ever worry about it?

Not much ...I've always managed to get what I need without much effort. But I desire happiness for my husband and he is always worried about money.

He worries about a lot of things.

I know and I wish I could get through to him about all of this stuff but he's very stubborn in his beliefs of reality. But anyway, I also desire money so that I can help the world. I've been reading A Diet for a New America[6] and I am disgusted with what we are doing to our animals. I want to change things. I want to do more than sponsor a starving child. I want to change it all. I want no child to know starvation.

Why would you ever feel guilty about desiring money for any of your reasons?

I don't know ...I just do ...maybe because I'm afraid that I will lose focus and become greedy once I have it. Maybe I'm afraid that even if I have the money to change things that I will fall short of my goals and fail. Maybe if I never have the money to do anything I wouldn't have to try, and thus fail.

Why are you so afraid of failing ...why aren't you more afraid of never trying?

I don't know.

Try to think of life as a game ...actually not a game because that would mean winning and losing. Think of life as a play ...and then literally play! Take your own advice and don't attach expectations to your actions...dreams...desires. Just be and do. ...make your own reality. You cannot fail because no one is judging you.

Except me.

Exactly ...you don't judge others so why would you judge yourself?

I hate that I do that.

Then stop. Money is what you make of it and so are you. Money won't make you greedy only you can make you greedy. Just because

---

[6] Robbins, John, Macy, Joanna R. <u>Diet For A New America.</u> Stillpoint Publishing. 1987.

someone has it doesn't make them greedy...You are not a greedy person so stop being so hard on yourself

Thank you ...I love you so much.

Chapter 10
What's Up With Fear?

Some people believe that to be the best person they can be is to rid themselves of all their fears and to live in nothing but love. And some people believe that in order to be human, you simply are going to have fears, that it is one of the polarities essential to living on earth (along with right/wrong; good/bad; up/down; yes/no; high/low; love/fear). And to accept fears instead of trying to rid yourself of them, is the best way to live life.

Question then is, "Upstairs, what's up with fear?"

Marilyn/Amboy/WA

Fear is your own personal attitude regarding life. When you are in fear, you are separate-or you think you are separate-from life. Everything in life is interconnected on all levels in ways you cannot, with your current mode of thinking, comprehend. So whatever you think, is felt by everything else. It might seem sort of invasive to you knowing that nothing is really ever private as you wish it would be. However, that is the way things are. In the greater scheme of things, this interrelatedness was supposed to be beneficial in that each part would recognize it was part of a whole; and each part, functioning at its best, would help every part to be their best. When one comprehends this small detail, assuming you have to make some kind of grandiose accomplishment to be important or appreciated, really just sort of falls away. I want each part of creation to understand its importance and its value and how no one part is more or less important than the rest.

Here is where fear comes in. If you do not feel you are part of the whole and that you are somehow unique and special and important; like everyone else, then you begin to put values and judgments on things. You begin the game of comparison. I have explained this before. A tree does not spend its time comparing itself to other trees. It appreciates completely all that it is and is the best tree it can be; whether that is small, large, gnarly, straight, short lived, long lived, it simply does not matter. You [humans], on the other hand, are always comparing yourself to one another. You judge each other by how you look, dress, smell, your possessions, intelligence, monetary value, and on and on.

You always live in fear of not having "enough" of something and that someone or something is somehow going to take it away. You fear time will take away your value as a human being, or your health, or your beauty. Other people will steal your property. You even consider your spouses as property and your animal friends. You pretend like you "own" things, when in reality you can't own anything. It is all freely given to you when you open your eyes to what is real. When someone threatens you with a gun, you are afraid this person may "take your life". If you were not afraid of dying, then this would not be true.

Marilyn, you remember your son in Boston in the park? A man pulled a gun on him and he just stood there. He said to himself that either the man was going to shoot him or not, and there was little he could do. He remained totally calm knowing he had agreed, on some level, to participate in this experience. The man's girlfriend finally convinced him to put away the gun. He did and they walked away. Your son continued on to work and continued to walk through that park, refusing to allow one person to change his life. He was living in truth. And probably that is what really made the difference. The man felt powerless and wanted to make someone else feel that way. However, your son would not play into his game. He remained totally calm, did not yell or get upset. It didn't work, and the man gave up and walked away. In the moment there is no fear. In the moment you can say, "Well, I am still alive at this second"...or "I still have food to eat" ...or "in this second I can still pay the bills."

Fear usually exists when you are trying to live in the past or in the future, which is impossible. You can only live in the ever present now. I am not suggesting that you deny your fears, because to you they are certainly real. It is just good to examine them and take them as far as they will go. You have a fear of heights. Why? Because you might fall and hurt yourself or die? You say you are no longer afraid of dying, so let that one go. You are afraid you might get hurt? Will you experience anything you did not choose to experience? No. So know that you will not draw this experience into your life unless you have something to learn from it; and release any more energy you may have around it. When you are faced with being up high again, talk yourself through it again and again. Ask yourself questions. Ask me questions and keep going until you have clarity. Eventually it may no longer be a fear for you anymore.

You see, even here it is the comparison game again. If you trusted that everything was connected, you would know that the earth you walked upon, the ladder, the house, the air, your shoes, are all alive too, and all a part of this moment. They would be assisting you in the process too, were you more aware. You could fall and not hurt yourself (smile). That is possible too, right? So, know fear comes from those feelings that somehow lead you to believe that you are apart from the rest of life. Each little being, each little part, really cares about you and your life and how you get along in the world. Because after all, they are counting on you too. If you could just grasp the concept that you are all part of an interconnected whole and you are all One. Knowing that you are all ONE, why not think and act in a way that encourages and inspires love, acceptance, cooperation, and understanding?

You can also choose to act in a way that encourages all those ideas of separation-which create fear of loss, wars, famines, and a hunger for something no amount of money or time will ever buy you. Living with your fears is a choice you each have to make, and I will not suggest that either way is right or wrong, or good or bad. It is a choice you have to make yourself, each and every moment you are alive. Life was created that way, to be matter of choice freely given to each of you. Decide what you want and then choose how to "be", in order to role model that and create that for yourself in the world. Love, God

Lennie/OH/USA

God, what is up with fear?

There is no fear. Fear is a state of mind. You can choose to live in fear or not, it really is up to you.

Ok, if it is really up to me—why do I choose to be afraid to live my life fully?

It is your light not your darkness that most frightens you. I've told you this before—many times—and you are starting to get it. I'm ALWAYS with you and LOVE is all there is, so live it. LIVE IT.

You make it sound so simple.

It is simple.

Ok, so how do I live it?

You live it by seeing—REALLY seeing—the god in each and every other person. Bless them and have ALL your actions answer the question "What would God do now?"

You've told me that before and it isn't very easy to do.

I didn't say it would be easy. It may be very difficult for some of you. AND it doesn't have to be. CHOOSE it, CHOOSE TO LIVE IT. Don't try—DO. Love IS all there is.

JofromAlaska

Hi God.

Hi Jo.

So, "What's up with fear?"

I gave you fear for protection and for relief. Yes, everything cannot always be love, even though that is a worthy aim to strive for if it is not overdone. "Be ye not perfectionists". I made you, you chose to be human. Humans are not perfect, so don't over-strive. It causes strife!!! Savor fear and all feelings. Appreciate them for what they are. Try (yes, I said "try") not to let them bleed over into every aspect of your life. If you can stay related to me—be in your higher self—there will be much less to fear. If I am your highest good, you need not have as much fear as otherwise. There are healthy fears and not so healthy fears. Those are for you to discern and determine for yourselves as you "remember". My love is always with you and it is also wise to have a healthy fear, a respect for things that can do you "harm". That is wisdom.

LittleSoul/Anadarko/OK

My dear and wonderful soul, fear can be perceived in any way that you like. And however you perceive it is neither good nor bad. What makes you feel true to yourself is all that matters. Are you experiencing who you want to be by having fears? Or are you experiencing who you want to be having no fears? I will tell you this: you will feel more calm and more loving for the less fears you have. You will live more peacefully and nothing will get in your way because you love everything. Everything makes you happy. Would feeling this make you feel satisfied or unsatisfied? That's all that matters about fear.

What do you feel? Remember that many things happen to you because you believe that they will happen to you. Do you believe that you will just have fears your whole life? Then that is true for you at that present moment. Will you someday believe that love is the only experience in your life? Then, when that someday comes, you shall have no fears. So, in summary, fear if it makes you satisfied. Don't fear if it doesn't make you satisfied. Do what satisfies YOU because I don't care. It's not like you will actually be harmed. Why would I harm myself? Remember that I will always love you from this moment on, and I have always loved you in this forever present paradise. But it is only a paradise if that is what you choose and if you choose to experience something different so that you can better know paradise, so shall it be, my wonderful division of me!

Tiaka/Japan

Fear is what has allowed us to feel the illusion is utterly real, and help us experience our vast range of emotions. It is a true gift from our source, god. Fear is what has led us in our continual searching for what we judge to be right or wrong, and thus grow spiritually in this dimension. Fear stems from love, the unconditional love that accepts all for what we are, god being in the body, experiencing separated awareness in the most wonderful game of life. We have forgotten the thankless task fear has accomplished for us? It has made this illusion so real. Ask anyone if their experience of fear, judgment, damnation, separation, loneliness, mistrust, longing, hatred, abuse, violence, anger, rage, envy, power, control, pessimism, sadness, etc., is real and all will most certainly reply that of course it's bloody real! Ask someone in the fourth dimension of conscious awareness and they will tell you it's not so real!

Therefore fear has given us such an overwhelmingly separated experience that love alone could never accomplish. Our source—infinite unconditional love, or god for short—knew all of this. But it was us, gods parts separated, who asked to experience the all that is. Our daily dramas we each face would not have the feeling of being so real, were it not for fear. Within fear we can experience both our evil and good nature. Once we love all of our parts unconditionally, we can create balance. We can see the perfection in all of life and learn not to judge any of it. Our choice, our free will! For some, the game has become so real they are lost in the hatred, murder, revenge, etc. Fear is what makes us turn and fight or run away. Without it, we would no longer wish to protect anything from destruction or even destroy at all. Once you see through the illusion you have created, you no longer experience fear. Accept it as part of your separated awareness and love it unconditionally. Fear is a gift from god. Worry not if the illusion holds no mystery after you realize that it is indeed a grand illusion. You can now see the beauty and perfection in it and begin to create anew. Once you feel your god consciousness return, there are countless other mysteries to solve and games to play. Worry not, for the magician has plenty of tricks up his infinite sleeves!

Patricia/NJ

Yesterday I felt balanced. Like for a moment in time I was not struggling. I was a person based in love, not fear. It was easy to be around people. They didn't bother me. They were fine all on their own because I was fine, finally. And this base in love was not these overwhelming loving feelings, it was a balanced being. Like when you have weight on a hand truck, you can drag or push it or you can find that exact balance point where the weight is weightless.

Yesterday, I found that balance, today I am back to dragging the load again. What got me to balance?

Some things cannot be accomplished by doing. What if you couldn't make it happen?

Well, it sounds like I can't. That's why I come to you for assistance.

Have you asked?

No, not really. Just knowing I want that. If I ask, then you may give it again, but I want more. I want that to be a permanent part of me.

It is. Your fears are the weights. Resolve the fears and limiting beliefs that add weight. Pretty soon you will be in the weightlessness of love!

SAM/Clinton/Mass

Fear is what you make of it ...and it is indeed something that is made in the face of challenges. Fear can paralyze you if you let it ...and that is the key. It is how you react to it.

God ...I think I have a good grasp on fear and its effects on people but could you allow me to speak with clarity ...so that others may understand.

Of course.

So let's take it piece by piece ...the first part of the question is

> *..."Now, some people believe that to be the best person they can be is to rid themselves of all fears and to live in love."*

First of all ...a person can't exactly rid themselves of fear as if the fear were fleas ...that really isn't how it works. It is however in a person's best interest to not feed into fear. For instance ...explain what happened last night, as it was not the first time.

Ok ...yes I let my imagination run wild sometimes. ...My husband was out playing softball and he usually comes home around 7:30. So when he didn't come home or call by 8:30 and 9:30 ...I became worried. I knew he probably just hung out after the game and had a few drinks, yet I couldn't get the image out of my head that he got into an accident.

And then what?

I let the fear take over my thoughts and then I started really thinking that he did get into an accident and what would I do without him and the more I thought about it the more sick I felt. I tried to read to pass the time because I knew deep down he just got caught up with his friends; but I couldn't stop thinking about how my life would be without him. By the time he did call ...I was so mad ...because I had been so worried ...And instead of being happy that he was OK ...I was mad. Thursday has always been his night and sometimes he does stay out late ...but I created this whole traumatic image in my mind and then went with it.

How do you see this as answering the question?

Well, because I know I do that ...And in other situations I see others doing the same thing. Like Norm worrying about money when right now we are OK...and even if things do crash down on us ...I know we will be OK. The fear is created.

Two people can go through the same thing where one is in constant worry and fear and the other just goes with the flow ...so does the fear exist? Only if you think it does ...In reality ...it doesn't. But you create your own reality and you see what you choose to see.

So the next part of the question is

> *"And some people believe that in order to be human, you simply are going to have fears, that it is one of the polarities essential to living on earth (along with right/wrong; good/bad; up/down; yes/no; high/low; courage/fear). And to accept fears instead of trying to rid yourself of them, that is being the best person one can be."*

To be human ...you don't have to have or do anything ...If you want to experience up ...well then you would then experience what down is in relationship to up. If you want to experience love then you would want to experience the opposite of love ...which is fear. Yet once you know what up is ...do you always have to experience the down ...to yet again know what up is? Only if you have forgotten what up is. The same is true for love. I tell you that it will serve you best to come from love because that is who you are. You are not fear ...yet people find it hard to understand that.

Why? I know ...I say that I have a pretty good understanding, yet sometimes fear does get the best of me.

You are a creature of habit and you have been taught to be fearful your whole life. You are now just remembering who you are ...and I rejoice as I feel you do also. You are evolving, which will take some conscious effort on your part to break free from your old habits.

That is so true ...even as I was worrying last night ...I knew deep down that I was focusing too much on my fears ...but I just couldn't stop.

Yes, you could have ...you chose not to.

I see that now ...but when you are going through it ...it's hard to see. Just like when Norm is fearful about money ...you tell him that the fear doesn't exist and that he shouldn't worry and that he should think happy positive thoughts...It doesn't work.

Because he is choosing to go through it and he must figure it out when he is ready.

I understand.

Let's look at another example. You are prone to ulcers.

Yes ...I know ...my whole life. And I never understood why, because I never considered myself a stress out person.

But you worried a lot of what people thought of you.

Yes ...I had, and still have, a problem with that. I don't worry about money or my job or my relationship with my husband ...rarely ...anyway. I worry about people and animals ...when they hurt ...I hurt and I worry about trying to help them ...constantly ...and then I worry about what other people think of me, which I know is so dumb. It's a bad habit, I know.

It takes control of your life when you let the fear in...you see that, don't you?

Yes.

Ten years ago ...you worried constantly about two of your friends who were going through some really tough stuff. Did it help?

No ...not at all. In fact, it made everything worse because I was so worried and wanted to help so much that I was afraid of saying or doing the wrong thing, that I did nothing and lost one of those friends. I anguished over it until a year ago when I searched her out and explained my actions. She mistook how I acted for not caring, and was so hurt that she pulled away from me completely. If I wasn't so afraid of being the perfect friend, I would have been a great friend. We are now repairing and rekindling our friendship, and I am now making a conscious effort to always be honest and up front, even if I'm afraid. It's worked out much better.

Love is all there is and if you could look down on yourselves from my perspective it would all be so clear to you.

Thank you ...thank you so much.

Chapter 11
Please Clarify Feelings

It's time to sort out the difference between feelings, emotions, observations, judgments, opinions, and projections. Here is an example. An angry man walks right up to me and looks me in the eye, not saying a word. I conclude this man is angry. Now, have I felt this man to be angry, have I judged this man as being angry due to his body language, have I observed this man as being angry, or is it a projection of my own anger that I have put on this man and maybe he is not even angry?

Question: "HELP! I need clarity on feelings and emotions."

LittleSoul/Anadarko/OK

My perfect soul, feelings are what you get right before you have an emotion. Let's say the person you have been going out with for a very long time is the person you want to marry, but your mate does not know this. One day, he comes up to you and says "I am so in love with you, you wouldn't believe!" Right after he says that, you FEEL excitement and love. These are feelings. Then, you get emotional.

Feelings are right before emotions because feelings cause emotions. Observations are truth about someone or a particular situation or situations. When you observe something about a person you are seeing their truth, although they may deny this observation just as many humans deny my observations. People don't see the part of themselves that you see. So it is very hard for them to believe that what you are saying about them is true because they have never experienced this part of themselves. They have never known this part of themselves.

Judgments are untrue thoughts or statements that you have about someone or a situation. They are things that you think or say that you could never know truthfully about a person. Let's say someone is talking to you and you tell them that gay people are perfectly alright. They are just like all of us but they merely have a few different sexual preferences. They completely disagree with you and think that gay people are going to hell. This is a judgment. How could they know that gay people are going to hell? They have no proof. They are merely telling you what they think.

Another type of judgment is if someone told you that someone or something should or shouldn't be a certain way. How can they know how things should be? They cannot, because nothing should or shouldn't be (for everyone). They merely should BE.

Opinions are what you think about someone or something. They are not observations because they may not be true, but they are your personal perspective about something. They are based on preferences. They can also be described as perceptions. Whatever you think about a person is your opinion/perception. If you think that tattoos are ugly, that is your opinion.

The man looking you straight in the eye may or may not be angry. Is he glaring? Is he smiling? Is he grinding his teeth together? Is he grinning? All of these are observations about him. What he is feeling or thinking depends on your observations. If he was giving you the "evil eye", then you perceive him as mad because you don't know for sure he is mad but he is logically mad (something he may deny). If he was merely looking at you in no way in particular and not saying anything, and you think he is angry, then that is your judgment. There is nothing telling you he is angry, and nothing telling you he is happy. If you can't know, it is your judgment. Just view everything he does as wonderfully perfect, and so shall it be!

Lennie/OH/USA

(To Llovit) I will admit that I didn't want to answer anything earlier this week—that fear stuff again—and yet, I did miss you and your question. Kind of interesting isn't it.

There were some other aspects of my journey with God that popped up this week. Maybe I was meant to deal with those first, so I would be in this space to answer your questions. I don't know—just I thought. This journey with God is soooo amazing!!!! It's EVERYWHERE in my life. I am having a hard time settling myself down to "do" my human job though. Who wants to do accounting when I can be remembering who I am?

Ok, let's see what happens when I ask God your question. Again, I'm going to type a stream of consciousness. I feel safe that way. Ok God, now the question.

It is you who place the anger on the man.

But how can that be so? Sometimes it is so obvious.

The man could be feeling many emotions. It is you who name it anger. In truth, it may be just as easily called frustration, hurt, disappointment. Choose any name you give to fear, for that is all there is there. It's your opportunity to be love back. That's who you say you want to be. You have been given opportunities just this week to see this question. And yes, it is perfect that you got the question today and not yesterday or the day before. You have learned a lot about fear this week. You have been listening more, not running away from it. And feel the strength.

Ok, I understand what you are talking about but we are not answering Llovit's question.

We're not?

No, I don't think so.

It is you who add meaning to everything. That man could have just as easily been seen as someone who's soul was in much pain. You choose to make it against you.

Oh come on, there have been plenty of times when someone has been really angry at me and there is no denying the anger.

Really? That is only one way to look at it. The man is...

The man is what? Come on God, come back to me.

Then don't send me away.

Ok, ok.

The man is in fear because his life is not going his way as he currently sees it. He can choose to be another way or not. His soul has a lesson to learn here. Lessons come in all shapes and sizes. Don't be so quick to judge others. Only see the love in them. Imagine what your world would look like if you lived that way.

That sounds very idealistic.

Yes, to you it is. It doesn't have to be that way. Listen, I tell you this: love, love, love. Be love at all times. That is the journey your soul wants to experience. This is the journey you are asking for. You know the way. I'm here with you always. With me all things are possible. If I am for you, who/what can be against you? You know this, choose it—or not — I love you either way.

JofromAlaska

Hi, again, God. I think we just answered this one! I am not currently confused about feelings, because when I get really confused I usually do my Feelings Exercise.

Sure, Jo.

So, God, sometimes we get real confused about feelings, I feel like they are part of my link to You, and Your assistance in my life. So, may we sort out the difference between feelings, observations, judgments, and opinions?

Hmmm....Feelings are deep, something I put into your soul, your essence, untainted, real for you, as you need to know/experience your reality at the time.

Yes, and as we go through life we are trained to lose contact with them?

Some of them. Observations depend on your perspective at the time and from the locations that they are made. Judgments are based on what you have accepted as your truths/your beliefs, whether you gathered those for yourself or merely accepted what was passed on to you by others and then subsequently adopted them as your own.

They take place in the mind and involve past learning. Opinions are your use of free will. Everyone has a right to whatever opinion they care to have on any subject of any person. Of course it is best, or nice, if they are aware that it is an opinion and are willing to admit that is all it is.

Okay, my friend asked the feeling question.

Thank you for asking. Your gut reaction may be right. Your feelings are always true for you—until they aren't. You are in a position where you are interpreting what you are observing. Your perspective here is of ultimate importance. How clearly are you able to see this person, their head, their heart and their soul? How much are you reacting to you, your head, your heart and your soul? What position was each of these in at the time for you and for him?

It takes practice and purity to learn to read those feelings, both yours and the other person's, and to tap into your natural empathy. You can feel it, and it [may] not be true for the man or for others. They may not be still aware of their innate feelings, be hiding from them, covering them up to protect themselves, and perhaps even [protect] you from them. As long as you feel it, it is true for you, and that is what you must go by.

I think in this case you are experiencing all four. If you felt it, you felt it. Did you feel it or just think it? Was there a gut reaction involved? Was there an empathy, a feeling? If you judged it you judged it. It was a mental activity in keeping with your past mental learnings.

If your perspective was one where you saw behavior that indicated anger to you, you observed it, whether it was there or not. You observed what you observed. You may have observed actions that looked like anger but weren't. We are really getting into semantics here, but your observation was one of anger. Whether what you observed was really anger or not is another question. What did your heart tell you? is a better clue. And, of course, your opinion is there to do with as you wish. You are of the opinion that he [the man] is angry. That might be a good place to start. You could even ask at that point, without getting your feelings involved by reacting.

You might say, "I sense your anger, am I correct?" You could wonder about it without immediately thinking it. You do not have to allow your feelings into the matter, because they usually bring up all kinds of old stuff that will involve judgment—right/wrong stuff. "You are doing this and you shouldn't".

I can think without feeling, or feel without thinking. I must think to judge. I can only observe that to which I have both access and desire to do so. I do not have to have an opinion, but I always may. This is a very difficult one.

Who cares which one you are doing? Why is that important? What is important is loving that person and yourself. Can you love them enough to remain open long enough to find truth? There is not just one truth. There is always their truth, your truth, and my truth. There are as many truths as there are people involved. It is important to come from your god-place with compassion for whatever is happening with that person. It might be nice to keep judgment and opinion out of it. Unless your gut feeling says that it is a danger situation. In which case, my dear, I hope your past experience and wisdom will guide you to make an adequately quick observation and enable you to judge what is best for you to do.

Marilyn/Amboy/WA

This man is merely being himself in this moment. He is in a place where he is perfect in the eyes of God because he is being himself, whatever that may be. I see problems arise when you find the need to use labels to define your world. Humans have evolved to a place where they find an inherent need to define everything, label it, and then also to decide whether what they feel, judge, observe, remember, etc., is "good" or "bad", whether it is "beneficial" or "not beneficial". What you create is a place of duality. God does not come from this place. God does not reside in a place of right and wrong. God loves unconditionally. God does not judge anything you do; as good, bad, right, wrong and so on. You have created all these things for yourselves. I feel that anything which causes separation from someone or some thing takes you away from God. God is inclusive, to use your definition. God includes everything. God includes the Mother Theresa's of the world and also all the murderers, rapists, warmongers, polluters, liars, cheaters, abusers ....and so on. So, you see, any of those things—and none of those things—connects you to God.

You can never not be in connection with me. Your feelings are not what connects you with me; and they are also one avenue to know God. Your judgments allow you to see yourself and to see me, too. Just because you do not like what you see or what you do or what you think, does not keep us apart. This journey you are taking with these questions is to discover how to connect with me in a way which allows you to know and trust what you hear. That, I believe, you describe as faith. So it is faith that will give you clarity and not labels. There are all kinds of people who hear the word of God. Some listen and some do not. You, Marilyn, strive to be in a place of neutrality, or non-judgment, and yet that is a judgment in itself, is it not? So just being and letting go, allowing yourself to be open to hearing what is said might be the place to be.

When you begin to define what you do and to desire to be in a certain place and not to be in another, you create separation. You then say, "When I am in judgment, I am not being with God. If I want to really hear God, I need to be free of having opinions; and I need to only be observing things." Does this mean when you are having opinions and judgments you are not connected to me? No, it does not. What are feelings? This again would require an explanation from you. You created yourself with senses.

You enjoy the definition given by William Blake (*The Soul of Sex*[7] by Thomas Moore) which says that the body is the soul manifest by our senses. This is a beautiful way of putting it. How many of your senses do you use all the time? I see that many humans go through life using a very minimal amount of these senses. A blind person can identify someone by their walk, their smell, their voice, their touch, sometimes merely the energy radiating from their being. They are often forced to utilize many more of their senses than you do. They do not judge a book by its cover. They do not go around deciding who someone is merely by how they are dressed or how they carry

---

[7] Moore, Thomas. The Soul of Sex-Cultivating Life as an Act of Love. NY, NY. HarperCollins. 1999.

themselves. They are more inclined to taste their food. They can usually tell what clothes they have on by the feel; whether they are inside or outside, the texture and feel of chairs and cement and the earth. Most people use their eyes to judge everything.

In your example, a blind woman may have not made that same observation. She may have encountered another human being without being able, in that moment, to paste on that label of anger. She may merely have engaged this person in a conversation. And in doing so, given exactly what that person needed in that moment not knowing where he was. From this place, this person may have been able to connect at a deeper level, below the surface of all those things you mentioned above. Of course it depends on each individual person and who they are. However, I was using a blind person to merely demonstrate that you were using your sight to define this person and asking me about what you perceived, and if I would clarify this for you. I view people more like a blind person, without any kind of label.

I do not feel you are any closer to me because you are experiencing feelings. You label your feelings, too. Describe feelings to me without labeling them. Perhaps the more appropriate questions would be, "How can I be more like God?", instead of, "How can I connect with you?" Because anyone in any state is connected to me, always. Everything is God, so how can you be more like God than to be who you are? Being authentic is being god like. What I see you desiring is to live in a world where people are more connected and more supportive of each other. A place where each person is being more authentically themselves and less structured by rules and ideas and beliefs created by a society, which you "think" or "feel" is not beneficial.

This is easy and yet possibly the most difficult thing you can do. Let go of every experience you have ever had. Release yourself from every single idea, every belief, every experience which you have had that defines everything and anything for you. Let go and let go and let go until you are nothing. Let go until there are no more definitions, no more labels, no more ideas about who you are. It is from this place of Truth you will discover yourself and who you really are. It is from this place you will discover the reality and the illusions you have created.

Since your birth into this incarnation you have allowed every being you have encountered to help define you for yourself.

Your parents and friends taught you their version of right and wrong. Society has done the same. You accepted or ignored or tossed away concept after concept, again and again. You, as a species, allow little time for original thought. You do not encourage anyone to define themselves. You have taken on layers and layers of stuff and accepted it as your own, simply because you knew no other way. My greatest joy is in creating; and in creating beings which can create themselves and their own creations. I desire you [to] create yourself in your own version of yourself and then you will know God—God creating God over and over again. My desire is that you be you, and from there all these questions will appear meaningless. Loving you, God

Patricia/NJ

For one, feelings are the universe's way to tell you, you are human; that you are on your path, you are walking with god. When one truly knows their own feelings and honors them—meaning: acts on them—then all the rest of life will fall into place fairly well. Each human has obstacles that need to be removed in their path as that is called evolution. Humans unblocking their path is essential towards the ultimate goal of reuniting and/or being one with god.

So, if one was to only act on feelings it may not be the most direct route if one finds s/he is traveling in circles and seeing the same scenery over and over. I say scenery, meaning: circumstances. If you create and recreate the same scenario, there is probably a belief that would benefit you to remove it. If you only followed your feelings and not removed the blocks, you would not get anywhere very fast. Now, if one chooses to continue in circles, that is fine, too. I don't care. However, you WILL care, as it is inherent in every one of you to push onwards to connection, love, peace, and joy. All of you desire to go to Seattle [a metaphor signifying a specific goal of life]. Some may choose to head towards Miami [a direction that seems to be moving away from that life goal] in this lifetime. Do not deny anyone their path as you do not know where they are headed in this particular lifetime. They may NOT be in a direct line to Seattle. Maybe they have previously chosen to get there via Chicago. Who are you to criticize their direction that is different than yours? That is arrogance and looking at life narrowly, through your own restricted beliefs and judgments.

SAM/Clinton/Mass

You have observed that this man appears angry yet it is your opinion that he is actually angry. You may be right, you may be wrong. Your opinion is based on past experiences, so is judgment. You identify the anger in this man because you know what it is like for yourself to be angry. Judgment and opinion are closely related. Both come to be from past experiences. The difference is this: to pass judgment would mean that what you think to be true, proper, the best way, is the only way. To judge someone, you are saying to that person that they live less than you in comparison to you.

Yet the truth is, everyone has their own path and is not to be judged, for it is [of] no use to either party. This is why I do not judge you. What good would that do me in accomplishing my goal? Opinion is based on past experiences, yet allows for the fact that there are other opinions that may also work well. To state your opinion you would state your past experiences to prove just that. Just as someone else would do if their opinion was opposite of yours. Opinions are subjective in that just as one can be proven to be just, so can the opposite. Observation is what is. It cannot be disputed yet observation can also be tainted by past experiences. This is observing with your mind and not your soul.

One person may be set on a negative path. Everything he or she sees around him is negative, validating the negativity. Is the glass half empty or half full? Perception. How do you perceive your world? If you perceive your world as one of love and oneness, that is what you will see and that is what will serve you best. If you perceive your world as a struggle and that you are alone ...that is what you will see. Does that serve you well? Take the angry man. Perceive that you are one with him and that you and he present love. You will see him in a different light. Ask him what he is feeling. He may be lost on his path. It is how you react to his observed anger that is important, not whether he is actually angry or not. Your soul only knows love. That is why when you are in love your soul soars, you can feel it. Anger directly confronts your soul, fights with your soul's purpose. Love is all there is, everything else is an illusion. Now to feel strongly about something is to feel passionate about something!

Passion expressed as love, and you will act accordingly. LOVE breeds love. Passion expressed as anger, and you will act accordingly. ANGER breeds anger. See love in everything. Express love in everything you do and you will create a loving world around you. When you are confused about what someone actually means, the most efficient way to find out if they are coming from love or anger or whatever they may seem to come from, would be to ask instead of judge. You are asking me for clarity, know that I am that angry man, ask away!

Anger is an illusion created from expectation. If you are angry about something it is only because your exceptions didn't match the results you were looking for. If someone is angry at you, it is because they expected something different of you than you gave. It is their expectation that created their own anger. Take away expectation and you take away anger. See this in your own life. When someone is angry at you, express love back. Stop the breeding of anger in its tracks and you will give birth to love. I am focusing on ANGER because that is what you used for an example, but I observe that you are looking for more than that. You are looking for guidance and for your feelings to guide you. Let your soul guide you ...get to know the pure perfection of your soul. This may take some practice for those who have been using their minds all their life for guidance.

When you are faced with a decision or problem, go within. Pretend that you made one decision and go with it. How do you feel? Pretend that you made a different decision and go with it. How do you feel? Your soul will give you the answer if you listen to it. When you feel your soul lifting, busting with joy, that is where your guidance is. Your soul is me and I will give you the answer if you listen. Do not think so hard. Ask. ...Listen. ...Simply Perfect!

Tiaka/Japan

Observations are that which we receive from our senses of touch, smell, hearing, sight and taste. Feelings are that which we receive after having observed. Our feelings can be used to react, to judge, enjoy, or fear our observations.

For example—the same knife can be observed in countless situations, yet evoke such an unbelievable amount of feelings in one person, let alone others. From the five senses we observe the knife is made of metal and wood. Its color is metallic silver. It is sharp to the touch and cold at the blade and warm at the handle. It smells of its properties and can be seen to have multiple uses. The feelings that are evoked from handling a knife are basic physical sensations. You could say the knife has evoked little feeling in you, especially if you were a child witnessing holding its first knife, without any prior information from an adult. Unless, of course, you relate it to past memories and/or your imaginings. If you have watched television, you may feel more if you have watched countless scenes of violence. The knife may repulse you, even though the knife is a mere kitchen utensil.

The knife, however, remains the same to your observations. The only thing that is changing are your feelings which draw upon past experiences of situations which involved knives. So why is it you feel so much when the knife is still, in fact, just a standard knife? Your feelings are what we use to emotionally express ourselves after any given set of observations. The feelings can be somewhat out of balance to what is observed; because people are using memories, expectations, predictions, perceptions and imagination to express their feelings.

The same knife used in a crime will provoke different feelings in the assailant and victim—one of power and fear. However, if the victim is a trained soldier, he or she may not feel threatened and feel his/her skills can disarm the attacker with ease. In which case the tables are turned. A feeling of power changes to fear and vice versa. The knife remains the same. The two people involved have perceived the situation differently now.

Now, what implications this has in daily life are when we have potentially difficult situations such as an argument with our boss. We can either react in a like manner with fear, anger and unresolved tension or we can come from a place of unconditional love. If you allow yourself to love the person no matter what you are observing, your feelings will be the same. You then cut yourself out of the equation and no longer feed the person's like energy. Fear creates fear and anger likewise, until the situation becomes dangerous or one person breaks down.

Once you see the source (god) is every being, you no longer react, because you are finally aware that the other is indeed you! Any emotion acted out is thus done to yourself, through the other. Would you prefer to love yourself in the other unconditionally, or experience fear and rage? If you enjoy the drama, there is no problem. Yet if you want to continue with your evolution (change, which is neither better nor worse, just different) then loving all others will help you immensely in this. Where once before you saw anger, fear, hatred, tension, jealousy and ill feeling, you can now see opportunities to heal, help, love unconditionally and [can see] chances to be compassionate if the other so desires it. This is the sheer beauty and joy of infinite unconditional love. It is yours to give, within any set of circumstances and observations. The illusion of fear and hatred has now disappeared. You no longer lock yourself into the dense emotional mine fields your feelings once brought you!

Llovit/WA/USA

Being empathic most of my life, yet not being conscious of it, I think it is essential that I sit down and answer this question myself.

With your recent discovery of your highly sensitive feeling based awareness, this question comes closer to home than many of the other questions. It is essential that this get sorted out prior to addressing other areas of your life, at this point in time. What the experiments and discovery (I had taken on some personal experiments leading to discovery of my empathic ability) has done for you is: one, to show you that there is much more to life than meets the eye; ...and two, take a humble approach, as this discovery [of being empathic] has thrown your belief system into a blender. What you have believed for years, now proves to not be true. It is one that knocks you on the ground in dismay, in overwhelm, in confusion, in fear. This, nevertheless, is a good thing. The more you come off of knowing it all, the more real, the more open to other ideas you are. When one's core beliefs are challenged, it always is a good thing.

Upstairs, about that, I was reading where it's best not to have ANY beliefs, or to have all beliefs. That sounds good to me. I would like more info on that.

As a human, it will be nearly impossible to have no beliefs. One must survive in this environment. The best you can do is to examine all beliefs. See which ones cause you distress, which ones don't. Become aware of your beliefs. Then you may do with them as you choose. It would be safe to say that a well rounded, robust living person has opened his/her mind up to challenge his beliefs and to accept the possibility of anything stated may be true, especially for the person doing the stating. All paths lead to me. All directions eventually will end up towards me. Not one is right, one is wrong. They all have vital elements essential to the believer of the path.

Ok, I have a question on 'all paths lead to me'. Does that mean that everyone's path in life will eventually lead to what? Connection with you? I thought we all were already connected with you.

Yes, you are, on the deepest level. It has become the goal of each individual to experience their connection with me on a conscious level. That is the path that leads to me. You can want all the cars, farms, houses, boats, you desire. But what each individual wants is to become, feel, experience, on a conscious level, that oneness with all things, which is me. That is what you most strive for. The urgings are there, deep inside every one of you. Some do not recognize the urgings, acknowledge the urgings, sense the urgings, on any other but the most remote level within them. For others, this is a driving force in their life.

I thought we all wanted LOVE.

And that is what you will get when connected with me, when connected with the all, with oneness. You will not know any difference. Meaning: you will not know other emotions, except through memory of them. This is why you were put here on this earth. To experience the all that life, living on earth at this time, has to offer. To have the duality of emotions. To experience it all. To be whomever you chose ...knowing that at one time or another you will eventually choose me. To be one with All That Is. Usually this is done when most experiences have been experienced. It's like playing in the sand. You can build a sand tree house—a sand castle—you can dive into it and destroy it. When you are through playing, you will then rake it over, watch the waves come in to even out the rough spots and wash it away. You are still playing in the sand. And that is perfect. Some people today have played enough and have decided to allow their castles to be washed away, and become one with the earth, sand, water and air.

Chapter 12
Today's Youth

LittleSoul/Anadarko/OK

At one point LittleSoul mentioned that he was interested in chatting with upstairs about youth in today's society. The conversations below were both online chats with LittleSoul directly, plus some questions and answers through email. (A side note, LittleSoul is a youth of tremendous connection and inner wisdom. He was 15 years old at the time of these writings—amazing!)

> **Llovit: I would like to have a dialog with you and your god here on this internet chat feature, LittleSoul, if that is okay with you.**

LS: Of course! Sometimes, questions may take more than right away to answer though. Some could get up to a few minutes. Also, well, god does not talk in words to me. It communicates in feelings.

> **Llovit: Yes, I understand, me too.**

LS: Sometimes, I put what She is communicating to me in words which do not mean exactly what he told me, you know? So sometimes, I may backspace some because she is telling me a new way to phrase it.

> **Llovit: I understand. That happens to me, too.**

LS: Perfect.

> **Llovit: Want to test this out a bit?**

LS: Of course!

> **Llovit: It's those youth questions I have a hard time with so maybe we need another subject ...hm.**

LS: Ok. That's perfect.

> Llovit: Oh, I got it. Sheesh this one is hard for me, as I have such judgment here. I have to stay observing/neutral. Perfect? I'm not so sure!

LS: *I am!*

> Llovit: God, when I see people on the streets, young people who are dressed in leather, chains, with orange hair begging for money, I cannot help but disrespect this style. Help me out with this.

Well, remember that relationships are very much based on perceptions. Your perception of them is "God, look at them! How can they dress like that?!" But that is the very same perception they have about you.

> Llovit: But the begging for money? I don't get that.

Some people desire to show their feelings rather than have necessities for an ongoing human body. They desire to be outrageous and let people know it than to live a long life. They are merely living in the present, not thinking about the future.

> Llovit: Is this their ego that is thinking this way? Fear?

Not so much their ego. Not fear either. They are merely expressing what they feel. They feel bright, so they have bright hair. They feel like rebelling, so they stray from loved ones and find out [about] life on their own. But all children are taught to live like this. For example, they see movies where people are on the streets in leather, chains, and have orange hair, and are having a great life. But those movies leave out something—money. This doesn't only come from movies.

> Llovit: So, what is the best way for adults/others to deal with this? Just let them be, learning on their own?

You may do that if you wish. You could also explain to them that when they see the TV show, it is not real relative life, but merely the glamour of it. They may see the kids that are dressed cool on the streets, but they don't see those kids begging for money. Understand?

> Llovit: Yes. And where do drugs/alcohol come into this picture? Do we just allow them to experience that, too?

Many children don't know much about drugs. They are mainly told to "say no to this" and "say no to that", when they don't even get the chance to know anything about it. Of course they are going to do something against what you say, because they see others doing that very same thing. But, if you give all the information about drugs and let them find their own answers to that, they may say "no" on their own.

> **Llovit: At what point do we step in and try to save them from a life of disaster down the drug path?**

Whenever you want. What do you think? Many parents have different decisions to make about that. Some parents have exceptional outcomes. Many don't, because they are only telling their kids to "say no!!! You don't have to know what they do. Just say no!!!!" The wise parent will tell their kids all the information they can on drugs. If their children grew up in this wise and open environment, they will go back to the parents (if they even go to drugs!) at their right time, when they feel they've had enough. If the parent thinks the child has had enough, so shall it be, but remember that the child may rebel later on..... ...

> **Llovit: Thanks god. I ran out of questions on this. Gives me a better perspective on this/these issues.**

You are truly welcome, my child.

> **Llovit: Thanks LittleSoul.**

LS: Anytime!!!!!!

A second chat took place between myself, Little Soul, and his upstairs within.

> **Llovit: One question I have is going back to parents neglecting their children. I can only imagine that parents are doing the best they can with what they have. The problem is when parents did not get the attention they needed as a child, then pass this along to their own children, these children/turned adults will pass this lack along to their own children. This perpetuates the cycle. I suspect there are other reasons or fears that parents neglect their children that run deeper than "not enough time". So, we can tell them all we want about spending more time with their children, but unless**

we change the fears inside, we will not really stop this insanity, will we? What can parents do to allow their children to act more loving?

Well there are many things, but I wouldn't just change the parents. In order for your child to be able to think for himself or herself, you must make changes in its whole environment. School must change its form of education, authority, and discipline. If churches have to be attended, commanding bible verses must be avoided, or merely taken as suggestions.

These are things which most parents wouldn't strive to do. The parents could act more loving and it would have a great impact. But unless the children CHOOSE to think for themselves and avoid fear (and divisions of it) on their own, it will be fairly hard for the parents to take this out of the children with so much fear in the world. There will still be hateful peers, judgmental authority (at school and church), and fearing environments.

All children are different, however. Some have stronger minds than others. They could reach enlightenment merely through their parents, depending on how strong (un-brainwashed) their mind is. And this starts with parents, in many situations.

If you desire to be more loving to your children and help them to think for themselves, spend as much time with them as possible, especially in the early years. Children need a lot of attention from the time they leave the mother's womb to the time they are in their teens. When they reach their teen years, they usually want to try to think for themselves. With all your love and support for everything the child says, s/he could be a very mature and loving teenager.

Many parents don't even listen to their children. Whenever their children comes up to them and asks them something which actually has a lot of truth to it, the parents laugh, actually laugh, at their children and tell them that this is not "right". The parents continue to neglect their children through their teen years, not taking much notice at all to what they think, but putting so many illogical untruths into their minds.

This affects the children in so many ways. This can cause the children to turn to drugs, violence, gangs, and so much more, merely because they were neglected from their parents. Now, the reason they turn to these fearing things is because these come from peers. These peers are actually listening to you and giving you some attention, unlike your parents who, when they don't even see it, are not attending to their children at all. Merely putting their say into their [children's] minds whenever they can, rather than letting them make up their own rules.

If the parents put most or all of their attention into their children with a completely loving and supporting attitude, the children will leave these gangs of violence and fear and keep their own loving thoughts. When parents find that their children are acting in this fashion, they feel the most joy and happiness. The parents who brainwashed and neglected their kids are unhappy that their children are actually wondering if they should commit suicide, and they wonder what happened (how ironic!).

They [parents] also argue, gripe and whine about how "stupid" the world is, and [yet] don't do anything about it. They may do this when their children are at very early ages, but these situations stick in their minds. I tell you this, everything parents say in front of their children, at any age, has an influence in their whole lives. If they gripe about the world, but don't do anything about it, their children could do the same, and more. It could make them subconsciously think they can be lazy, [so] they don't get a job, they don't take care of their bodies, etc. Your child sees and does everything you do. It's all they learn from. You know the saying, "Do what I say, not what I do"? It's impossible for children to do that if you say opposite of what you do, because the children see the irony of the basis of your life. But all of this is very perfect! It just isn't loving.

> **Llovit: Wow, I think you've just answered my other two questions, which were about how to get children to act more loving, and how parents could be more loving.**

I could say more, if you like.

> **Llovit: Sure! Most parents need all the help they can get!**

Ok. Now, parents can give their children anything they want, as long as what they want is natural. From birth to around age five or six, and even BEFORE they are born, you are giving them tons of things which they never would have thought to ask for. This is because you spoil your kids. Everyone does it, it just depends on to what extent you spoil them. Spoiling your children means to give your children things they don't ask for. Now, when you spoil your kids to such an extent that you do, you are putting unnatural desires into their heads.

You blow your whole bank account giving your children what they didn't even ask for, and then when they want even more—because they unconsciously know that if you gave them this much, you can give them more!—you can't give it to them because you don't have the money. If you only give children what they desire, you will have enough money and maybe even some left over! You and the children are happy and satisfied.

Also, for your children's sake (if you want them to be loving), be open about sex! Don't tell them to "put that away" or "stop touching there". Instead, tell them "that is interesting, isn't it?" and "enjoy!" Shutting sex out of kids' lives is what puts them in psychologist offices and buying impotency medicine. When you make them ashamed of their bodies, you make them ashamed for their lives.

Now, like everyone, they are doing nothing wrong or right. They are merely doing what they were taught to do. Their parents taught them to act this way, and their parents' parents taught them to act this way. They cannot help acting this way unless they can overcome their teachings. This has been happening for a very long time and so it was meant to be, and it is perfectly grand. It is just very primitive.

LS: Thank you for that. It is great I have my own counselor in my heart communicating with me whenever I desire.

I'm not only in your heart, my perfect soul.

And then there was a third chat we all engaged in...

> **Llovit: God, it seems that some children get all the love and attention they desire, yet they end up in jail, causing trouble, traveling down destructive paths anyway, no matter how perfect the parents seem to raise them. Why is that?**

That is a very good question which does not call for a long answer, compared to how long they have been. Parents are not the only people children pay attention to. They also pay a lot of attention to the world. They watch cartoons, which portray violent activity, and the parents think nothing of this. They think, "Well, it's just a cartoon. What could it do?", when it does a lot depending on how your child chooses to perceive the world.

Not only do cartoons have "innocent" violence on them, but so many movies have continuous disrespect, violent behavior, and/or "bad" language (I'll get to the "bad" language discussion in a moment), children are told that the president [former president Bill Clinton] is a great man and should be respected, and then they see him lie about something as completely natural as having equal love for more than one person. (What does that say about the world?) So, that situation is planted into their brain, "If this man is respected by my parents, maybe I'll be respected if I do what he does." So, they lie also. They see people robbing banks on TV, and they act it out. They are also told that they can get away with it from peers, and so they learn from that.

Children also have tremendous pressure from peers. Children can only hold so much pressure. They have to be "cool" or popular. Whatever you call it, you have to be the same as everyone else, or you are not accepted. Don't try to show any originality! This pressure can only be held in for so long. Then, BOOM! They blow up and beat their wives, children, or their neighbor, for being different themselves because they have to be the same too!

All acts from people are from personality, and this is built from environmental energies, negative or positive. Now, parents can teach their children to not allow this pressure to increase. They can teach them the outcomes of certain acts. They can also be careful of who they tell their children to be like. (Some things parents tell their children do matter as to how their personality is).

Of course, the learning is up to the child, depending on how close to the end of its soulic cycle it is. If you are closer to the beginning, you will learn mostly from watching people, without working out the logical in your mind. If you are nearing your end (almost ready to begin yet another cycle), you will know the logical and the loving, and you will act on that. Whatever you choose, it's wonderfully perfect!

Llovit: You wanted to discuss "bad" language?

I didn't want to (I'm choosing to!), but it would be useful as to the outcomes of what you teach your children. Parents and other authoritative figures constantly tell younger ones not to say cuss words, use "bad" language, or use any kind of originality. And then, the children hear all these words on almost every TV show! This causes much disillusionment. How can they listen to you when they see almost everyone doing it anyway? People learn from experiences, whether it's from their own or from other people.

Llovit: Great!

You're welcome, my wonderfully perfect child.

And a fourth exchange:

Llovit: There are so many different youth circumstances possible, from child prodigies to starving children, from enlightened youth to schoolhouse murderers. To fully understand youth, I think we need to delve into the facts about reincarnation. Correct me if I am wrong, but my understanding on why youth are whom they are has much to do with the decision made of the soul between lives, and prior to birth. Can you explain this process? And the agreements that must be made with other family members for the soul to experience its choice?

This perfect process gets so very complicated. It really isn't a process. A process is something that takes certain steps in a certain order to get a certain outcome. This simply isn't possible in the irrelative world because time does not exist in an irrelative world. It cannot.

There are basically two circumstances a soul would be in. One is when a soul chooses to experience itself with it's "past body personality" (watching over family, friends, flying around, having fun, etc.) and the other is when they have chosen to experience themselves as fully aware of their oneness with everyone and everything. I will explain the situation with a fully aware soul first.

Let's say that you wanted to move your arm to pick up a glass of water (and of course this is the arm of a completely healthy person). When this arm moves, there are no other physical parts trying to stop it, and there is "no thought" to it. It simply happens. This is a mere glimpse of what it is like with a fully aware soul entering a body. It simply happens. It knows what it chooses to experience, but there is "no thought" to it (there actually is a thought to it, but I use "no thought" in terms of my analogy). Every other part of this whole infinite soul automatically agrees because it is all one thing merely having one part do a particular job.

Now, with the soul who still chooses its "past life personality", it is about the same way except there is a little more of a desire for particular parents (desire is the closest word describing this feeling). He may "desire" to be a she. She may want her past life sister or brother to be her parent. In any situation, all of it is perfect, and I will do nothing but agree to that.

> **Llovit: Why would a soul choose to experience being a murderer, starving, or have disabilities?**

Well, let's start with the basics. You cannot experience one certain thing without its opposite for comparison. You cannot know love until you have experienced fear. If you only had love, you would "forget" how good it feels because you wouldn't have anything to compare it to. Now, you are a soul that has been experiencing good love after comparing it to having money stolen, your car wrecked with only liability [insurance], and other things to that extent. Now, you want to experience a greater level of love, so you choose for yourself a greater level of fear for comparison. You may choose to be a murderer, to be raped, starving, or in some other perfect situation to that perfect degree. So, whenever you are ever in a situation where it seems it won't be any better for you, think about how good it will feel surrounded in ease, warmth, and love (whether that time comes in physical form or otherwise).

> **Llovit: Hey, now you aren't going to tell me that the way to experience grand love is to be down and out, raped, victimized. I don't believe that. I have been down and out and victimized and I don't experience love to much of a degree at all. Besides, that would then say that the ones who have had an easy life only experience love to a mediocre degree. That I don't believe either.**

If you don't believe that, perfect. If you ever choose to believe it, perfect still. I did not choose this for you alone. You chose to experience the absence of love so you could see how great love could feel. Do you think I would force this way against your will? You are mistaken if you have this thought. Forcing of another's will is not a godly act. Any being that does so is a perfect impersonator helping you experience another grand part of your loving self.

You have been victimized and you don't feel well about that. Is that the fault of the victimizer? Does the victimizer control your emotions? No, you do. You are allowing yourself to feel bad. When you are done with this level of anguish, you will choose for your self a situation which brings love to you. This will make you react in a grand way whether this situation comes in this same physical body of yours, or after. If this situation comes to you in this physical body, you will have a choice, through ignorance if you would like, to compare the situations. If you wait for this love and relief until after you leave, you will compare the situations because you will know how great it feels to compare love and the absence of it.

Okay. Someone has led an easy life. Maybe they don't choose such a grand level of love at that time (you have infinity to experience anything you want, anyway). Maybe they are experiencing this grand level of love in this life, while their aware part is comparing it to a past life. There are many perfect reasons for this. I have given you two. Give your self a different reason, if you prefer. If you do, it has already happened, it is happening, and it will happen, in a most grand way.

Again, you don't have to believe this. This information is out of one's very open and spiritual mind. Make up your own rules, with anything and everything. That is what many do, anyway. That is what I encourage. Search, learn, and create. I love you for it now, and I always will without doubt, with perfection and infinity.

> **Llovit: Say a soul decides to experience blindness. So, the child is born without sight. Now, in his/her childhood, modern medicine has discovered a surgery that will bring sight to this person. Was the decision made prior to birth that the person would be blind for only part of his/her life, then this discovery would happen and then s/he would have sight? Or, was the decision of blindness made prior to birth, and then changed as the person became older and maybe at that time, the soul decided that it was time to experience sight? I guess the question is, does the soul make these types of decisions throughout all of our living life, or just between lives?**

Why can't it be both?

> **Llovit: I guess it could. How?**

It could be a continuous decision. A soul could choose this healing in life so it could experience grandness in physicality rather than waiting until after. It could be an immediate choosing if it isn't ready to end its physical life to feel the ultimate feelings. This is yet another very small look. Vocabulary is so very limiting with irrelative worldly situations, but that is just as it should be. The moment you understand absolutely everything, is the moment you leave relativity, and that is ultimately perfect.

Llovit: What if I desire to experience understanding everything and staying in physicality at the same time?

When you understand everything to its greatest degree, you will not have any desire to stay a part of your physical self. You will understand that there is no reason.

Llovit: What if I want to help others understand?

You will see perfectly that they will get to that point in good time. Of course everything you are saying is possible, but very rarely happens. It would not happen on earth because everyone on it has chosen to experience a lower form of evolution. It would have to go against everyone's choice, and one being does not disagree with itself. That is left for relativity—physicality.

Llovit: What about Jesus, Buddha, and all the other masters who have religions in their names?

They understood a great deal, but not everything. They were helpers of evolution, not gods.

Llovit: How could they be helpers of evolution when wars are fought in their religions—in their names?

They did not start their religions, nor did they start such close-minded cultures. Their followers (of many years after their times) did this perfect work.

Llovit: Ok. I understand a little more now. Thanks!

You are truly welcome, my perfect division of me.

In even another chat, LittleSoul (a teenager) offered this conversation he had with upstairs regarding his school system.

I can't believe how disorganized my school is.

Obviously someone can, since it is so. The principal thinks it's pretty organized, or he would change it in your school, anyway, and as much as he can. Everyone has a different thought about this. Some have more REALization than others, but the disillusioned are doing as much as they can with the information they were given. They were taught the children are the disillusioned, and so they apply that to their present life. They have been given the REALization information, but they have lived with the disillusion longer, so they automatically apply that. Unless this realization "theory" can be proven to them, they probably won't ever see it in this life of theirs.

Now, there are people who see this. Teachers at your school REALize it. There are two reasons why they don't "come out of the closet". One, they fear they will be called evil (or something negative) for their new age thoughts. And two, they don't think they are right. They have this aching feeling to tell their truth, but society has created their fear that they will ruin everything, when everything is going down anyway!

With the subject of youth, Patricia submitted these words of wisdom about teens and sex.

Patricia/NJ

When a boy wants sex with a girl at a young age, no behavior is a pattern as of yet. The girl has the ability to teach at this moment. Since the boy wants sex and the girl wants love, the girl needs to teach the boy about love. She will learn sex. He doesn't need to teach her that. Sex is one single act. Love is many faceted. There needs to be a distinction between the two.

The girl does not know how much power she has, as a teenager, as her tendency is to follow the boy's lead. And if the boy is not taught to love, will lead right to sex. The girl needs to realize what she wants, or she will never get what she wants. If she lumps it as 'love', look at what aspects means 'love' to her. It's time to educate them [the boys], now. When she determines that love means taking care of, carrying books, whatever she determines what love means, let her define that. And in all of that defining, it breaks love down into certain behaviors that the boy can do. And it teaches the boy to do certain loving behaviors that may eventually lead to what he wants, which is sex.

Let's take an example. A boy and a girl meet. A boy wants sex, a girl wants love. If pushed to define what love means to her, she may say, "love means I see him after school everyday", "love means he calls me up everyday", "love means he pays attention to me and looks me in the eye when he talks", "love means he's not interested in other girls", "love means he asks me out on dates", "love means he doesn't want to be with anyone else".

When broken down in this aspect, this is what the girl wants. And in order for the boy to get (or think that he is going to get) what he wants (sex), he must perform these duties. A boy without this discipline is no better than an animal. He will have sex because he wants to and he will find any available female that will give it to him. This sets the stage for possibly the rest of his life—or until he is forced to change. So, at this young age, it is essential for the girls to know what they want and what is important to them. Because what's important to them now is what's going to be important to them later. There may be some added things that they didn't know or realize at this young age, but this is essential in training the boy to give more than sex. And to GET more than sex. And it is training the boy to WANT more than sex.

If left undefined, the girl will say, "He loves me and I'm going to have sex with him." And the boy's mind says, "I'm hot for her, I'm hot for her, I'm hot for her", because the girl has not given him any behaviors to perform prior to [the boy] getting his physical needs met. If a girl and a boy come together and are taught properly, it will benefit the rest of their lives to know how to treat the other person. I say these things, as it is so essential that the girl temper the boy. Because the sex drive in the boy is so strong, it's essential to get it tempered at this young time. When the girl has all her needs met and is convinced that the boy is now loving her because he as performed all these behaviors, then it is okay to further the relationship and have sex with him.

Cynthia Attar

This is magnificent wisdom and fodder to chew on for both parents and youth. Thanks much to LittleSoul for his extra effort and timely wisdom; and thanks to Patricia for her take on teens and sex.

Chapter 13
The Significance of Family

Most animals raise their young well. When able, the offspring leave the nest to find their own way in life, never to see their parents again. It is nature's way and perfectly okay. People are a bit different. Many parents care for and raise their children. When able, the children leave the nest to find their own way in life. However, quite often the children stay very connected to their siblings and parents, even in a damaging family. Some adult children would rather do as the animals and move on with life being happier alone, or creating their own families. But societal obligation says that we humans must stay connected with family for the rest of our lives.

Question: "Upstairs, can you address some aspects of the significance of family after children are grown, please?"

Norma/Mexico

Dear Father, what is the importance of the family as we grow up for us as evolving beings?

It's a connection, it's a lesson of love you may want to remember. They are there because you have chosen them to be with you. Ask yourself why did you choose THIS family instead of another?

Okay, why did I choose this family instead of another? Because, we have been connected for centuries? Because they are, have been, and will be, teachers, reminders and schoolmates?

That's right.

But you say time doesn't exist.

It doesn't, but this is the illusion you believe in. In fact, this family IS always part of you, in this past-present-future that is your experience.

SAM/Clinton/Mass

Family is the closest thing that most people today have, that links them to their ancestral past. Before technology, towns [people] were closer; as media, computer technology, and video games weren't their main pastime. People knew their neighbors. Children played outdoors. Dinner time was family time. As technology becomes our entertainment ...imagination dwindles as does close knit relationships. Passive activities, where individuals hardly communicate with another for hours on end, are becoming the norm. Society has become so focused on the independent individual that we have isolated ourselves from one another. This is why it is hard for some to grasp the concept of oneness. The family (in some way, shape, or form) is important in all stages of life.

God ...what if our family life has been abusive (mentally, physically, sexually). Should we seek out close friends to become our family?

There are no shoulds and should nots. You are all one, so whether you share blood or not does not mean you NEED to do or act or be a certain way. Yet if your immediate family has been abusive then you might find happiness in forgiving them, understanding them, remaining open to them, for when they are ready. In the mean time ...let go of notions of how they have affected you. Don't live in the past ...analyzing why you are the way you are. You are who you are. Live in the now. Let go of negative energy as you have given it more than enough attention.

I am just starting to do that God. I blamed my mother for my lack of self esteem and eating disorders for the past 28 years. I made myself the victim and so I remained a victim. It wasn't until I saw that I had a choice between passing the blame or taking responsibility for my own actions and feelings that I felt cured of my ..."baggage". I see my mother in a whole new light and instead of being angry at her ...I now feel sorry for her, for she is still wrapped up in superficial things that just don't matter. This subject of family is so close to home right now, as my parents are headed for a messy divorce that threatens to separate my family. I am in the middle, as always. I clearly see that my father's actions are out of love and my mother's are out of fear. So what do I do ...how can I help?

By being an example of who you want to be. That is the only way.

Is it, God? Or is this the only thing that is coming to my mind?

You can't change others in the way you wish to change them if they do not wish to change themselves.

I know ...but I feel helpless.

You help your father a great deal. He wants help ...he's open to it and is seeking it ...thus he is receiving it. As you wish to help him also you are succeeding in providing it to him. Your mother is not seeking help and thus she is not receiving it even though you wish to help her.

But God, I really think that she is mentally ill and that it's not her fault that she is the way she is. As much as I have blamed her in the past and still get angry at her now and then ...I think that she can't help herself. Things are so crazy and I get so emotionally involved. I would like to tell her exactly how I see things, but she never asks. She seems to see how everyone else creates their own reality but yet she blames everyone else for hers. It's very frustrating. My father has health problems that I fear will become fatally worse if and when this whole divorce happens and the family business is torn down. I try not to worry, but I find it almost impossible sometimes.

LittleSoul/Anadarko/OK

Do you think that after children are grown, they automatically need no more help about life—about experiences? Even so, parents also like to be informed of their children's lives. They might like to know about present-day evolutions that they didn't get to experience in their "primes". Family brings that certain sense of union and love into your life that many cannot yet get from outside family friends. Outside family, friendship usually brings more of an impersonal love than family. They can also have more understanding of your feelings and emotions because they felt the same way themselves (which is a branch of the wonderful understanding of genes and inheritance of them). But some do not prefer this kind of closeness and therefore grow away from the interest of their parents. Maybe they don't want help from others, so they decide to live life independently. Maybe the family never really was close anyway, so you never knew this closeness to begin with. There are so many perfect possibilities. So, depending on your preference, there could be very little significance of parents, or they could mean everything in the world to you. I shall do nothing more than call it perfect and guide you through when asked because I love you unconditionally. You can never be harmed. That will never change.

Llovit/WA/USA

Family is a series of people that you have agreed to grace the planet with through the lives of all in agreement. When one dies, then their agreement(s) has been fulfilled for that lifetime. There are prearranged circumstances to work through and learn from all through your life. If family was meant to just raise children there would be more instinctual drive like in animals. Impregnate, birth, raise a short while and never see again. Humans, on the other hand, obligate themselves to a lifetime of challenges with family—of course this includes adulthood and seniors.

But what about us who are very distant to relatives? Why?

When one chooses to be and remain distant to family members, then either all is finished with you and the other, or the family is postponing the inevitable, the prearranged agreement. If two people in a family feels they are through with their lessons and agreements, especially at a young age (20-40), then it is most likely that there is much more to learn with family. If there was no more to learn, said family members may only have been acquaintances in one's life, or short time friends that move on. Since one has been 'selected' as family, there is probably more to learn. One would benefit to continue contact and communication with family members to continue with the prearranged agreement and learnings through the years together. Stopping this process midstream only postpones the lessons and possibly holds them over to another life to finish. It may prove that another (friend, stranger, etc.) may help to work through some lessons. However, many lessons in family need to be worked through with that particular family member as that member needs the learning also and that is the prearranged agreement.

You, specifically, have chosen to not follow through with your agreement with certain family members. The disharmony within is felt by all as they are at a loss to resolve or learn or experience specific circumstances and either must wait for you to come back or attempt other ways for these learnings.

Chapter 14
Serving the World and Creating Our Life

These subjects weren't actual questions to the group. At one point I requested if anyone had an additional important message they wanted to share with the readers of this book. Lennie and SAM took me up on my offer. Here are their dialogues on subjects of their choosing.

Serving the World

Lennie/OH/USA

God, how can I, Lennie, best serve the world and all its problems, right here, right now?

You know your answer to this.

Prayer?

Yes.

Ok God, some folks are going to read that and say, "Prayer—yeah, right—what a cop out."

Yes some will, and you can bless them and ask them to join you.

People aren't going to get it, God. I used to be such a doer, now I just tell them I'm going to pray? Won't they laugh and wonder just how x, y, and z are going to get done?

Let them laugh. It just may be part of their journey to "get" just what prayer can accomplish.

This just seems so forced to me—this conversation.

You are trying too hard.

How do I lighten up?

You just do. Let go Lennie, let go and let the energy flow through you.

So all you wish for me to "do" right now is pray, right?

Yes, and be the nurturer that you are. Your role has shifted, my dear (a new baby arrived on the scene recently). It is time for you to be the love in the world that you ask for yourself daily. And for you to do that right now, you must give up the doing. There is nothing for you to do except become closer to me, trust me. You think prayer is not good enough for you? You don't yet realize the full power you have in that regard. Would it not benefit the world for you to realize that full potential? You know you are a powerful prayer [person who prays], you can even say that is who you are—you have come a long way with that—have you noticed?

Yes.

So take it further, develop your abilities. Constant prayer—isn't that something you ask your life to be about?

Ah, yes, I remember that. It seems so long ago.

Well, here is your chance.

Man, people need to be careful what they pray for!

Yes they do.

Let's go back to constant prayer—won't people think I'm being holier than thou?

So what? Who cares what others think?

Well, I do.

Yes and that is also part of the lesson, for you to remember to not care what others think of/about you. Look at the flip side, Lennie, you just might be an inspiration to others. They just might say, "Wow, if she can do it, so can I."

Fear just swept right through me with that one.

So what are you afraid of?

That it will work.

What will?

My prayers.

Ok, let's play with this. Let's say that your prayers do work, and you know they do. What could possibly happen?

I would have to acknowledge my power.

Yes, and what is fearful about that?

I'd be like you.

Yes, and what is fearful about that?

I would have to give up my story that I'm not worthy. (The sun just came out and shone on my desk. To me, that is always a god sign— the sun shining.)

Yes—let your light shine, Lennie, let it shine. Type in Marianne Williamson's words (in *A Return to Love*[8]), "Our deepest fear is not that we are inadequate. Our deepest fear is that we are powerful beyond measure. It is our light, not our darkness that most frightens us."

So Lennie, you don't need to know the particulars anymore. You don't need to be involved in the decision making anymore. You don't need to do the planning or execution anymore. You get to visualize it and cause it to happen through your "symbolic" power, which is prayer.

Wow, you make it sound so easy.

And is it? Let's define living your life in constant prayer.

Well, I would define it as living consciously in ever moment, choosing to come from love and not fear, from spirit and not ego.

And I ask you, is that easy for you?

---

[8] Williamson, Marianne. A Return to Love. NY, NY. HarperCollins. 1996.

No. I have come a long way with living my life consciously and I still have much to learn.

You will, you will. Be gentle and give yourself time. And take the time to acknowledge your growth along the way.

Self-Creating Our Lives

SAM/Clinton/Mass

Dear God, I love you. Thank you for that which I know.

What do you know?

I know that I am creating every moment. I know that every moment is a gift. I know that you have sent nothing but angels.

How do you know?

I have experienced it.

You have experienced it? How may others experience it?

All I know is the path I took. I researched dozens of books on a wide range of beliefs, ancient traditions, spirituality, philosophy. I had many doubts, yet an inner pull towards reading ...reading a lot. When I wasn't reading, I thought about what I read. I analyzed it and looked for clues in the outside world trying to make sense of it all.

Did you make sense of it all?

At times it seemed I did. There were moments of complete awareness that when... not only did I make sense of it. I saw clearly that I am part of it, all the time whether I knew it or not. Then there were times of great doubt—self-doubt. Who am I to think I am so powerful? Who am I to think that I am not only equal to God, but the same as God? At those times I feared I was going crazy.

What did you do at those times?

I cried sometimes and I asked you for help—to show me the way—to show me what was true, what was real. I fell back to reading again, as when I read books that spoke to my soul, I felt safe because they validated everything I knew in my heart to be true.

Then what?

Someone close to me—my beloved dog—got bone cancer. It was diagnosed in a very late stage. She was in terrible pain. I knew for two years that something was wrong with her but the vet missed it every time I brought her in, insisting she had arthritis. I became angry at you because the vet missed. I became angry at you because this did not make sense to me. I had read a book on healing and convinced myself that to make sense of it all I would heal her. If I was like you, I could heal her. Every moment I focused on pushing out the sickness to make room for health. I did not sleep. I begged my husband to have an open mind that miracles do happen. It had to happen. In the end, I chickened out. I was afraid I was wrong and I did not want her to suffer because of me. In the end, I held her head. She looked deep into my eyes as they administered the needle. It was as if time had stopped and we were looking into each other's souls. "I am so sorry!" I said with my heart to her. It took awhile to stop blaming myself for failing her.

You never failed her. You freed her and you freed yourself.

Thank you. I miss her, though. I freed myself?

The moment you freed yourself from blame, you freed yourself from all blame—your parents' divorce ...your mother's sickness ...your eating disorder ...and all the pains around you. It was a great moment, indeed.

It was tough.

You are a creative being, but it is impossible to create what you desire when your thoughts are all self-defeating. You said it to yourself that day. You thought it...you said it...and you wrote it down to remember. And I am reminding you again...right now, that the world around you is the product of the energy you send out—thought, word, deed.

Yes, I tested it. I thought, "I am creating five thousand dollars easily and effortlessly. I wrote it down in several different ways.

Then I went about my business awaiting a clue to what the deed would be to manifest the $5,000. We were moving and looking for a house...we were sure that we found a town and a builder to build our house, yet the appliances wouldn't be included. My husband and I would have been tapped out for cash, figuring new appliances might cost an extra $5,000. We hadn't mentioned it to anyone that the appliances were not included when we got a call from his grandmother warning us not to put the appliances in with the mortgage. She offered us $5,000 as part of the money she had set aside for us in her will. This was all within a few weeks of the original thought. It was [as] if I was looking into the eyes of God when my husband gave me the news.

What did you realize?

I realized that there is nothing to fear ...that I am creating every moment ...and that you have sent nothing but angels. Since then I have seen the same results almost instantly. Whenever I have a thought that I am deliberately manifesting, I link it to the original thought of "I am creating five thousand dollars easily and effortlessly" because that is something I know came true.

My warmest appreciation to SAM and Lennie for the inspiration and timely nudge-to-action these messages provide.

Chapter 15
Oneness—Asked by Tiaka/Japan

Tiaka/Japan requested a question on oneness to be answered by the group. We know through our studies that we humans are one with everything and everyone. Many of us don't quite grasp this concept of oneness except on an intellectual level. I also see where living our lives in separateness, rather than oneness, creates much difficulty on a day to day basis.

> *Question: Is there anything specific that we can do or be to further ourselves and other people along to fully embrace, feel, and truly know this oneness with all?*

JofromAlaska

Hi God.

Hi, Jo.

Nice to be back at this again. By the way you made a gloriously beautiful day here yesterday!

Thank you, I know. And you are so welcome—so glad that you bothered to notice and especially to enjoy it so much. That is what life is all about—to experience and enjoy all the innuendos. By the way, I also like your idea of a praise or thank you chain to compensate for the heaviness of the prayer chain that you are on. People, (some) think I am only here to help them with problems and only come to me in that respect. Yes, I am here for your thanks and appreciation foremost. To have you share with me your joys and appreciate your blessings!

Thank you. I feel that very much in my heart. Well, I am here today, prompted by Llovit and Tiaka, to bring you this question.

An excellent question—my thanks to Tiaka, Llovit, and to you, Jo, for bringing it to me. It is important to bring as much as possible to me, until you truly have the "mind of Christ", so to speak, for those familiar with the Christian Bible. When you know me well enough that our minds are one, you no longer exactly have to bring things to me. Though anything brought to me is always welcome and gratefully received. Nothing from my beings is beneath my reception. As to oneness, that as I said, is a wonderful question.

I know that the importance of oneness has been becoming evident to you, Jo, and this question might have come from you—except that I did not give you the gift of asking questions this well! Ho, ho, or perhaps I did give it to you and you have not yet availed yourself of it! Oneness, you with me, my son with me, all with me, and then all with all—my, my, what a wonderful concept. I must congratulate myself. The wonderful simplicity, simpleness of it. And the wonderful types in all the earth, the coral and hydra, the smallest of animalcules that gather as one into larger animalcules. How fascinating. How important. How wonderful. Don't you just "llovit"? Ho, ho. And find it endlessly amazing? It all works, and it works so well. Then there is my big brained folks who love to do it themselves, to improve on my everything that they/you can get your hands on, so to speak. Paying no attention, really, to how things have been set up to work; because you are all creating your godness, but avoiding the principals, the natural rules, trying to make a different game.

Well, Jo, as you often say, God knows what he is doing! I know what I am doing. If you will learn me, learn the natural and work with me rather than against me, amazing things are possible. Anything is possible. And if you work against me, ghastly things are also possible. You have choice—that wonderful, terrible weapon of freedom. The question is, do you have to learn everything by trial and error, or are you willing to trust?

And another question is, have you been taught to trust, by living in a trustworthy world? Have your parents been trustworthy? Are you being trustworthy to your children, your friends, your selves? My, my, this is all such an eternal question.

Oneness?

Yes, oneness. Perhaps the whole answer, the only answer. Someone of you realized once, "United We Stand, Divided We Fall". "Wherever Two or More are Gathered Together". "Together", "United", what wonderful words. Today you [people] celebrate Earth Day. The idea of concern for the unity, the oneness of the earth—wonderful concept, a wonderful place to start. And what about the oneness of the universe of all—of God, which is all? What about the oneness of oneness?

What can we specifically do or be to embrace it?

First it must become real and important to you. You must learn to love it and to see it. Have you experienced oneness? Anywhere? When? Who? Was it good? Did you appreciate it? Did you enjoy it? Did you realize the importance? Why did I create oneness as the basis of your creating? Is it not the epitome of feeling? Or the oneness you feel in worship or love of me? Is that not ethereal for many of you? An epiphany? Come to love oneness as you love me, as you love yourself. As you love others. As you love anything. As you love. That is a good starting place. Enjoy.

Thank you. I will.

LittleSoul/Anadarko/OK

My wonderful Llovit and Tiaka, don't try to further people and force them to evolve faster than they have chosen because that would go against their will. (I'm telling you not to do this because it doesn't reach the outcome you are desiring.) If you keep laying the concept of oneness on them when they completely disagree with it, they will only get agitated; which is an outcome far away from the outcome you wanted for them. You can tell them the concept and allow them to see the peace it has brought you. That would be one of the best ways to see if they would change. But if they do not change, do not worry because they merely have not yet chosen to evolve to that level. Call them perfect and leave them be, because they are not ready to experience understanding of that kind.

Thank you.

You are welcome, my perfect being.

Patricia/NJ

Now, for what it's worth, life doesn't suck. It doesn't even like to be described as having a label, a judgment. But then again, and I say this loosely, life has found a way to begin the next sentence before the last has ended. [The] life you know is the life force in all beings. The will to live, the will to grow, evolve, connect back with God in the oneness of all oneness's. This is the calling of all humans. This is the inner core that once all the outer layers of fear are peeled off, one becomes this ball of love that also strives to remember and connect and keep the human body.

As long as one has the body to occupy, one will feel ungodly. It is inherent in the plan—the big picture. Once the body is taken, then the veil of forgetfulness sweeps over.

Why do we do this, God? Why is this part of the plan necessary? Why do we need to forget and then spend all subsequent human lives trying to remember?

God wanted to experience everything and could not if he was only love. So he created human with no memory (by the way, animals are aware, they have not forgotten) of being god—or animal. This puts them into the duality of good/bad, fear/love, right/wrong, etc. Only in this duality can one experience the opposite of who they truly are, of that part of me. And only in this duality am I able to experience the joy of the human world and all its duality.

Marilyn/Amboy/WA

Marilyn, oneness is a concept difficult for humans to understand, comprehend, and accept totally and completely. You see, you were created as individuals; each one to be different and unique, and you are. This is what separates you. This is where the beauty of life originates in its creation of itself; each time completely new and completely different. There are no two identical blades of grass, snowflakes, trees, or human beings. There is a uniqueness and difference in each and every part of life. There is also a Oneness, a Wholeness, which you comprehend on an intellectual level, and have difficulty taking down into your soul. Why is this so difficult, you wonder? Well, if you take it all the way down into your soul, and into each cell of your being, your lives would be transformed, and you would have to take the issue of "responsibility" to a new level. I would like you to understand what this means.

Say, for instance, you suddenly accepted the fact that each and every part of life, from the smallest atom to the largest mammal, to the earth itself, to the Universe, all played a part in the creation of the whole; and each part was significant. Each life and each death had meaning. Could you live with this understanding the way you view life at this moment? Consider for a moment, that EVERYTHING IS SACRED. Every step you take, beings die. Every breath you take, life ends and begins. Each and every movement you make, each and every thought you think, each and every action you take or choose not to take, affects all of life on some level. Tell me, could you take another step?

Would you know what to do and what not to do? Would it be likely that all your old fears or doubts or questions would suddenly rise to the surface? It is an excellent question and the answer is not an easy one. Letting go and flowing with life, following your inner guidance can lead you in the direction you desire. Contemplating this issue can become an immense challenge to some. In your every day life of eating, bathing, walking, sleeping and so on, you come in contact with literally millions of forms of life; and some of them die because of this contact. Some are also born and some continue to live. You decide all this. By your actions, you choose which lives will end and which will not. This can become an awesome responsibility. Ask yourself, how would your life be different today if you knew this fact? If you desire not to kill, then how could you live and not do this? It is literally impossible. Death is a necessary part of life. You decry the taking of life when it is intentional, be it an animal or a person or a tree in a forest, and yet you do this all the time without consciously being aware. So now you become aware. How do things change? You are certainly not meant to cease living. There are billions of tiny beings which are alive because you chose to have a body. If you choose to die then they also will transform into something else.

Where does responsibility end and begin? In order for you to begin to grasp the nature of this situation, you can begin to view all life as sacred; for without any part of it, the rest of life is diminished. It may continue on as you do when other species go extinct, and yet your lives are diminished, nonetheless. Become more aware of all the different kinds of life which surround you daily on your body, your clothes, in your house, your yard, your car, your animal friends (and on your animal friends), plants, nature and so on. It is impossible to consciously be aware of all these forms of life; however, intention is a powerful tool. When you begin to become aware of how many beings depend on you and how much you depend on all these other creatures for your daily survival, you can begin to sense the true sacredness of life and each and every moment you choose to live in it. I do not choose to take out parts I don't like and throw them away. This is not how I operate; and yet people, humans, often wish they could get rid of all the "weeds" in their lives—the things, situations, people in their lives which are too much of a challenge. There really is no such thing as a weed in your garden or in your life. Each part is necessary and serves a purpose.

When you begin to recognize the sacredness of all life, and release the need to call things "weeds", you will begin to touch into the enormity of what you are asking to feel and understand. It is a lifelong process, and one you must choose to make. It is really not something you can teach someone else or even share. You can ask other people questions to stimulate their own thoughts and begin their own series of questions. Your job, however, is to take this comprehension deep down inside of you, and see how it changes your life. See if you feel differently before you take a bath, knowing that with that act some lives will end. Will that affect how you bathe? Would you want to thank and recognize those beings before you do? I am not making suggestions here, only asking questions. When you vacuum and clean your home are you aware that you are intentionally taking lives? Is there any kind of reverence given as you go about this process? I could offer you a book about this subject and it could probably change your life. I would suggest this, to begin with.

Each day, take a few moments to think about all the myriad of forms of life with which you will come in contact that day. Express your gratitude for their lives, and the part they play in your life, whether or not you understand or even comprehend the part they play. This is not necessary. Strive to see and understand that each part is sacred and each part deserves a kind of reverence for all the rest, including yourself. You are God. Everyone is God. Everything is a part of God. You like to separate things out into sacred and not sacred, but what parts of Me are not sacred? You take my body and transform it into a nuclear missile. Does that mean those parts are no longer sacred? Why? Is that not separating things out and not understanding they are part of the whole? Everything around you is part of Me, including each and every part you do not like or would like to "weed" out. I will tell you this. When you can begin to see the sacredness in all things and all forms of life, then you will truly begin to see yourself reflected back in all you see. You will begin to realize the enormity of what you have created and that it, too, is all a part of you.

You are not separate from the pollution, from the killing, from death. Only when you can truly see and feel yourself as part of everything you truly do not like and do not think you can understand, will you be able to feel yourself a part of all you love and appreciate. Oneness is not something that opens the door into another world, it is a way to understand yourself. In reality, what you are truly asking Me is how to feel that Oneness inside of you. How to bring together all those different parts of yourselves, the parts you like and the parts you do not like, and often don't recognize. For life "out there" is merely a reflection of each of you as individuals, unique and different as you may be. Again, look inside and as you see all parts of yourself as sacred, the world will bring itself together and Oneness will become all you see. Look in the mirror and caress your face, as if you were caressing the face of God. Make this a sacred act, doing it reverently. For you are caressing Me when you caress yourself. Begin with this act of reverence for the love and beauty you truly are, including all parts of your being, and you will be on your way home to the feeling of Oneness you seek. Loving you always, God.

Huge thanks go out to Tiaka/Japan for coming up with this oneness question. It really shows the depth and intricacy one can achieve in their communications with upstairs.

Chapter 16
Why Do We Fear Death?

Question: It seems like many of our life problems come from the fear of death and dying (some say the fear of suffering prior to death). We know so much about peace and love in the afterlife, why do we still cling to this fear of death, and how can we get past it?

SAM/Clinton/Mass

People fear death for many reasons. For some it is the fear of the unknown. For some it is the fear of leaving unfinished business or loved ones behind. Some can't conceive of who or where they will be when they die.

God, I don't think I fear my own death as much as I fear the death of the people I love. Maybe it is because I have yet to have a close friend or relative die and the thought of losing—say my husband—scares me to death. I trust and have faith that when I die, I will experience bliss and I trust the same will be experienced by those I love. I guess it is a selfish fear that I don't want to deal with; [and] how hard living would be without these people.

That's understandable.

I'm understanding that we create our own reality with our thoughts and actions. What if my constant, needless worry sends these messages out into the universe and my fears transform into reality?

That may very well happen. The key word in your question is "needless". Those who live in the now do not worry over such things. Those who worry, often see their worries come true—which in turn validates that their worrying was for a reason. The answer is to not worry, to live in the now, to appreciate and love openly these people around you as if you knew that you might not see them again. In this way you will be sending love out into the universe instead of fear. Out of love comes peace, happiness, and well being. So many people hold back or take others for granted out of fear. Unfortunately or fortunately, when tragedy strikes, fear immediately disappears, things become more clear, priorities change, anything seems possible.

Why?

When you lose someone you love, your ego takes a back seat and your soul takes over. Your mind is tired of thinking and lets it happen without a debate. Nothing matters to those who experience a trauma—at first. People may say, "that person is in shock" ...or "...is numb". Perspective can change in an instant.

Does this have to happen? I know everyone dies eventually, but it seems that tragedy symbolizes that there needs to be a change, as so many people change for the better after a tragedy. Why is that?

People tend to wake up after a tragedy, that's all. They're going to work or whatever—stressed out about this or that. They're not happy with something and then bang, nothing matters. They wake up and see instantly whether they are on the right track or not. Things matter. Not the things that a lot of people worry about. Why don't you fear death?

I don't think that I do, but if it were staring me in the face maybe I would. I just think that whatever pain I feel will not last, and what I experience after death will be beautiful. I trust in that. I trust in you. Plus, I trust that whatever reason I do die will be to benefit someone or something else.

Why do you think that?

Because I am here now, and I am awakening. I haven't done anything amazing in this world yet, but I feel I will. I want to do your work in some way, and I trust that you will guide and protect me.

I will. You have nothing to fear. My advice is to live in the now. In the now, you are alive. In the now, your loved ones are alive. Life is a nanosecond. Your love goes on without fear and you will always be close to those you love because you and they are the same. You and they are connected.

I love you, ...that is why I don't fear death.

Norma/Mexico

We know SO much about peace and love in the afterlife, why do we still cling to this fear of death and how can we get past it?

As always, it's up to you. You are the one making decisions all the time. It doesn't matter what you think about death, it is one more illusion. Everything around you is illusions—you have made them up. How can you get past it? Choose to do so. You are little kids playing this game. You can choose a happy end.

LittleSoul/Anadarko/OK

You say you know so much about this peace and love, but do you know the peace and love from personal experience? You may know about the thing called peace, but do you know your Self to be at peace? You do not if you must ask this question, as wonderful and perfect as it is.

Also, many people fear anything that they don't know anything about. Paganism (or any religion other than their own), homosexuality (or any sexuality other than their own), or African Americans (or any race other than their own) are in this wonderful category.

There could be many reasons why people choose to fear rather than love these things they know nothing about. How they were taught at their younger years is a very popular reason at this present time; along with religions that people are apart of and groups that they spend time with.

If you desire to get past it, simply turn to love. Live for and with love. Think loving thoughts, no matter the situation.

Are there exercises we can practice to get to this loving state?

Meditate on love. Make positive or loving affirmations about your Self, others and other situations. You can think about death, and say to your Self, "This will be a grand experience for me. I will truly love this situation which will bring me great joy." Practicing tolerance can be helpful as well.

What about those of us who have never experienced love in this life who have no money for counseling or anything?

Then that is their physical life, and it will be a much more intense feeling of peace, joy, and love when their body stops working than if they led a physical life full of love and happiness.

Sounds perfect to me. That is wonderful, truly wonderful.

Marilyn/Amboy/WA

Death is not an ending point, it is only a point of transition. If you watch a flower grow and bloom and die, you are watching its transformation from one form into another, or transition, if you wish. Then, depending on the plant, it may completely wither and "die"- only as you know it to be—for it merely is changing form again. It never really "disappears" from view. You just perceive it as dead because you ignore the rest of the process. The plant, let's call it a daisy, composts now by the participation of many different kinds of beings, which are all very "alive" in regards to how you view life. They are very much alive. And through this transformation, the daisy now transforms into the soil and the process continues over and over again; with a seed taking nutrients from the soil, up into its body and soon everything is interconnected. The rain and sun and even you, walking by or admiring the flower or talking to it, become part of it. Humans have a very narrow range of focus. You limit yourselves so much by you, what you choose to perceive and what you choose not to see. You "perceive" the plant or daisy as dead, and in reality, only the form you were familiar with is no longer visible to your eyes.

This is true when a human dies, when an animal dies, when anything dies. The form you are used to seeing ceases to exist only because you do not perceive "the rest of the process". Let's look at animals who seldom fear death. They understand their being-ness, their place within Nature, that they are part of an interconnected whole. An animal dies and you bury the "physical" body. It decays—the part that you perceived with your limited point of view—and continues to live as it decays, and so does that which you do not perceive. If humans were to begin to utilize all their senses and all their abilities of observation, they would recognize that the soul/essence of the Being is often still around. It often lingers for a while, being with you in your time of grief. Whenever you are thinking about this animal, the energy and soul of this being is with you. In this place after the physical body dies, and when in physical form also (and this is another story), time and distance are meaningless. The being is not confined by a physical body and can be many places at one time. Sometimes an animal has been with you before and it remembers you from lifetime to lifetime. There is a continuity for them. When humans incarnate, they often forget their past lives because it could interfere with their processes in this life. Because of this, you often feel that when you die that is the end of your life. In reality, it is really another beginning.

You will be reborn again into this world or another. Creation and creativity continues forever and nothing ever really dies; it just ceases to exist for you because you believe it does. How you get past this, is to change your ideas and beliefs about the world and how it functions. If you continually believe that death is the end, that you have only one life to accomplish everything you ever wanted, that you are a limited being, you will continue to experience these fears and continue to have the experience of suffering. In reality, you are in a physical body to "experience" life. You experience many things like sitting in the sun, feeling its warmth, enjoying its light, feeling grass beneath your bare feet, a butterfly landing on your nose. You experience these things. You do not say, "I am sun, I am grass, I am butterfly", because this would sound silly. You do say, "I am happy, I am sad, I am a mother, I am a carpenter, I am suffering", and so on. You get all caught up in your emotions and with identifying yourself with these and other things. How might it be different if you said, "I am a human being experiencing being happy." "I am a human being experiencing being a mother." "I am a human being experiencing suffering." You would look at things in an entirely different way. You could experience anything you want, and know that it would leave you just like when you step out of the sunlight, or the butterfly flies away. You could experience what ever you wanted, without worrying about attaching to it or even having to identify it in any way.

Imagine you were here to experience life and all you created, without attachments. I view everything as perfect. I do not put value judgments or labels on your life experiences. If you just said you were having an experience and felt it fully and let it pass through you, there would be no fear, would there? If you didn't label things as good and bad, as peaceful and chaotic, as wonderful or horrible, there would be nothing to fear. Suffering simply would not exist anymore because it would become only one of many experiences in life. Humans fear what they do not understand and you simply do not understand death and what a "wonderful" (to use your terms) part of life it is. What an experience to be reborn from one form into another. There are so many, many things available to all of you which you keep away, simply because of your need to define and structure your lives into predictability. Every single moment you are given examples of how that is really impossible, and how it isn't what is true. If you just were to let go of all of this and trust that life is filled with miracles and possibilities beyond your imagination, you not only would not fear death, you would begin to enjoy life at a different level, and perhaps desire to make the journey a little longer. Learn to "experience" life without labeling it for a while, and soon death would only become something else to experience, not something to fear.

Chapter 17
Animals, Nature, and the Earth

Before we parted ways in this Q & A project, I could not miss an opportunity to have a chat with Marilyn about animals, nature, and the earth since they are very much a valued and essential part of our lives. Marilyn, such a clear communicator, is vitally passionate on these subjects. I requested of her to submit her god-self writings in this realm for final words that we can apply in our lives now and forever.

Animals and Nature

Marilyn/Amboy/WA

Some people say that the evolutionary path is one of reincarnating to higher and higher forms of life...only going one way—up. Like a moth becomes a bird, which becomes a dog, which becomes a human—humans being the highest form of life. Some people say that one can reincarnate as anything, that there is no 'higher' or 'lower' forms, and a human can come back as a rabbit, a horse can come back as an ant, etc., as needed/wanted.

> Question: "So, which is it? Linear evolutionary path upward or mix and match evolution?"

Evolution happens according to each individual species. Each species, including human beings, can make changes in themselves. It is a matter of choice. No one species actually causes another species to go extinct. It is a choice of the individual species that conditions are such that it no longer wishes to reincarnate into a certain environment. You view it as permanently gone and yet it never really dies and can reside elsewhere in other dimensions or come again into yours if it chooses. It is also a matter of choice within a species and within an individual, as to what it chooses to experience. Many species enjoy staying within the character it has chosen. Some cats enjoy being many different kinds of cats. Some beings like to always be large, so they are a large dog, or an elephant, or a whale, instead of being a mouse or an ant. All of life is creative and it is this creative spark that guides one from one place into another. Some animals enjoy changing each time into another animal. Some like to be domesticated and others prefer to live away from people.

People can choose to become animals and animals, people. Most often this occurs because of a desire to know the other more intimately; or to learn lessons that have not been learned by other means. Within plants and minerals there are not as many variables. A tree does not think and wish about becoming a human being or a cat or an ant. It is satisfied being a tree. It is composed of similar particles or cells and so when you eat an apple, it actually experiences life as a human, or a bird, or an ant. It does become you. It therefore experiences all these things in a different way. Everything is interconnected to everything else. You like to isolate things out and try to separate life into individual packages to suit your needs and your limited capacity to understand. This exists, of course, only because you utilize so little of your brain's incredible capacity. If you used it all, these questions would become meaningless. You stick to your theory of evolution and keep trying to prove it only because it provides you with an excuse to live your life as you choose; and you can feel you are the supreme being. Any idea about the equality of all life puts a weight of responsibility on your shoulders which you do not want to share or recognize. Thank You.

> *Llovit: When I talk to animals, they tell me that one of the reasons they are here is to help us humans evolve, especially pets—those close to humans. I don't know if this is accurate, but it does bring up the question as to why do some animals chose to be near humans. Personally, I see animals as so much more evolved than we are, it's like they are choosing to be around first graders when they are skilled enough to commune with their own college level! Is human evolution important to animals/pets? And if so, why?*

I smiled when Marilyn read this question. There is no such thing as a silly question, and yet coming from a person like you, whom I know well, it seems a little silly. All of life on your planet is interconnected. I would hope that this is one thing you have learned from all your communicating experiences with animals, nature and even your car, your television, your house plants, and so on. There exists an interconnectedness beyond what you can even comprehend, since you use so little of your brain and all the incredible abilities that lie latent inside of you. You are an incredible, limitless being capable of much more than you might imagine.

Anyway, as I have explained earlier, a hair falls off of your head onto the earth and composts into soil. And then becomes part of a worm who eats the soil, and then part of a bird who eats the worm, and part of a tree which the bird poops on, and so on. You eat an apple and it becomes part of your body and later some is released when you defecate back into the soil again.

Scientists now agree that thoughts are alive and have energy. When you are angry or mad, all those around you are affected by this energy you are sending out ...other people, your house, your house plants, your animals, and much more. So think about this for a moment. What you do every day affects everything around you and, due to the interconnectedness of all life, eventually [affects] all of life on your planet, including nature spirits, fairies and more. If you use chemicals and pollute the ground or water, millions of life forms, including human beings, insects, animals, and more, are affected. When you care for the planet and begin to see all forms of life as sacred and you take care of yourself and live in a way that contributes to the well being and health of this planet, all life benefits from your actions, including those animals who choose to live with you. When you heal, they rejoice. You have all lived many lifetimes. Nature and all it contains is constantly aware of this interconnectedness and acts accordingly to create balance and harmony; with the exceptions being where humans have intervened and made this impossible. Human beings are the only ones who strive to isolate themselves from all that surrounds them, and to pretend they have no effect. This way they are relieved from taking any responsibility for their actions. Of course a human being could not understand an animal's actions in wanting to help human's evolve regardless of the sacrifices they must make to do so. Because few of them [humans] would be willing to do the same thing for the good of the whole, so to speak. All these animals understand that when they help humans become more of what they are capable of being, of remembering their "essence" and who they really are, that the animals and all other forms of life will benefit and rejoice from this awakening. I am hoping you can understand this and if not, then ask more questions and I will try my best. Love, God

Humans: The Earth's Steward

Marilyn/Amboy/WA

In regards to nature and the earth, Marilyn had this important message for all of us today.

God, please share with me what I and other humans can do to help co-create a healthy vibrant environment, one that nurtures all of Nature and all Beings that dwell here with us, from the smallest to the largest of Beings.

Marilyn, the world is at your fingertips. You can, with your thoughts, affect all of life around you. While plants and animals have their own sense of being, they respond to you and all of life. Without judgments and attachments to outcome, they remain in the ever present now, enjoying, appreciating whatever comes their way. If a blade of grass be eaten by a cow, stepped on by a deer, or cut by a lawn mower, it FLOWS with its experience, joyously being itself, living, dying, or transforming into part of another being, as in the cow's stomach.

Life is not waiting to happen, worrying, planning, scheming. Life "is" all around you. What permeates all of life around you is love. The sun does not withhold its radiance in anger, nor a bird sings its song in resentment. Each is joyously being itself. It does not wish to be something else. Each part does its best, thereby creating the "wholeness" you find yourselves living in. Each part recognizes it is part of the whole. Everything cooperates and balance is achieved. This, despite all humans have done, because the environment "responds."

How can you assist the process? Guess!! Of course by being the best you that you can be. Let go of your desires or needs to change or control anything or anyone else. Have no expectations of others. Release all your assumptions. Then life flows with you and you with it. Then the give and take is always mutually fulfilling.

Of course the opposite is also true. When humans experience feelings of scarcity and not having enough or they want to take away from others, control or manipulate other beings or situations, the flow is altered, shut down, pushed back, or directed somewhere else. Feelings of separation and longing, pain and suffering, do the same. Taking out your anger and rage against another causes change. Anything which does not come from, or originate from, a place of Love affects all Life around you in different ways.

All life around you is constantly and consistently working to create balance and harmony. It responds to whatever happens without attachment to the outcome, without a judgment about what was done. Its only desire is to be the best it can be in any given moment; thereby helping to assist the whole in becoming the grandest version it can be. If you had hateful feelings out into the forest, it must absorb and transform those feelings. When you get angry, resentful, feel your desires are unmet in some way, all those thoughts and feelings have a direct impact on every being that surrounds you, be it your car, a desk, your clothes, a tree, or a flower. Your animal companions often absorb vast quantities of these kinds of energy and often become ill because of this. They are only attempting to create balance within their environment because that is their job.

Imagine what happens when you cut down a forest, or even till the soil to plant a garden. What about putting in a new sidewalk or building a road? In Nature, there is a cooperation among species, among beings, a knowing and cooperation. Most often when humans react to a situation, they are completely ignorant of all the forms of life around them. They create havoc, chaos, death and destruction by their thoughtless actions. There are millions of forms of life wiped out in a moment of time. Homes are destroyed, ways of life forever altered, a part of the whole is disrupted or completely destroyed, and you are not even aware of the devastation you just created. It is as if someone came through your own neighborhoods with a bulldozer which was twenty stories high and completely destroyed it, killing people, destroying all the homes and streets and stores and all forms of life, to construct some huge thing. Think about all the massive deaths that would occur, all the pain and suffering. How many people would be dead or maimed and dying? Think how your lives would never be the same or possibly cease to exist. These other beings were so huge they never even noticed you at all. They were completely unaware of what they had done and continued to do. I want you to really think about this for a moment. Can you even imagine what that might feel like? Everyday, as you carry on your actions in your daily life, you live among millions of beings, microscopic, small and large, and you act without the slightest bit of awareness as to their lives and what you might be doing to them.

Nature does not think like humans. Nature does not react. Nature responds with love again and again and again. If it did not, there would be little left for you to enjoy and appreciate. If Nature reacted by no longer growing, or if millions of species of plants and animals merely disappeared from your planet, you could not survive. Nature is here as your teacher. It responds, again and again with love. It merely adopts, transforms, dies, changes from one thing into another. Life continues. You continue to have food to eat, clothes to wear, natural resources to use.

Now you have taken over so much of the planet's surface that an imbalance has occurred. There is no longer enough nature to maintain a balance on the entire planet. In some areas, the damage you do is more permanent and without an effort on your part, without human interaction, balance and harmony can no longer be maintained or created again. It will take a conscious effort on your part to change this.

Marilyn, the more love you have in your life, the more love you express and share with others, the more you come from this place, the more you add your healing energy to those around you and this includes all forms of life. You see, you are a part of the whole as well. Each human being was created to play a part in the role of creating balance and harmony and the ever constant creation of life in this dimension. You just went to sleep. You forgot. You stepped out of your role of cooperation and communion with all of life and went in another direction. You began playing another game which includes manipulation and control. The only thing you need to recognize is that you can never win this game. You depend on all the other parts for your survival. You need food to eat, clothes to wear, homes, and shelter. More and more of you are looking for places out in nature to retreat to, or spend time in, or build your homes in. You recognize at your deepest most level what really and truly nurtures you and what has meaning. For without your environment, without all the beings which help create the place you live, there would be no meaning and no reason to go on.

Imagine a world in which you no longer tasted the millions of delicacies you call food? What if you no longer enjoyed the sun on your shoulders, clean water to drink, the songs of birds, a forest of trees, the ocean, rivers and streams? What if no more flowers ever grew, and all you ever saw was asphalt. Suppose the color green disappeared? Would you want to live in a gray world? Think about it. Be quiet, go inside, and think about the things that are truly important to your life. What gives meaning to your life? Do you enjoy having friends? Do you appreciate eating wonderful food, watching the sun set, listening to music, inhaling the fragrance of the air after a summer rain, enjoy flowers growing in your garden, a walk in the forest, clean air to breathe?

Do you appreciate every piece of clothing you wear and all the lives that went into creating it? Know this. Cotton does not grow in isolation. Cotton grows in soil in which billions of tiny forms of life exist, and which all cooperate to create a balance and harmony in which plants grow. Then there is the sun and rain, the moon and the stars, which all play a part in this dance of life. Various insects, birds, animals, all contribute to the process of the growth of this cotton plant. Few of you yet understand how birds singing actually creates growth in plants, for instance. Or how the sounds of insects and other beings greatly contribute to the health and vibrancy of all of life. You know so very little and yet to act as if you know it all.

What can you do to help your environment? You can wake up. You can begin to develop an awareness of all the forms of life which surround you each and every moment of your life. Recognize their life and their need to survive, just like you do. They are part of the whole. When you act, act from a place that recognizes the sacredness of each and every part. When you go to construct a building, connect with nature, state your intentions, co-create what happens next. You are totally capable of so much more than you might ever imagine with your limited imaginations. Working together with those around you, you could create so much beauty, so much magic your hearts would overflow with love and adoration for the magic of it all.

When you accept your part and you come from a place that always is striving to be its best, magic always happens. You just let go and go with the flow of life, and everything you might imagine, can really come true. The secret comes from a place of allowing and response and not from the need to have things your way. Breathe into this moment, and come to recognize all it has to offer you, and then respond with your love. Life would change and you with it.

I am in awe of Marilyn's ability to come up with such insight and depth of conversations. My deepest gratitude to her. Marilyn's submissions have really opened my eyes and changed the way I live my day to day life. I now scoot a bug out the door instead of squashing him, tell the trees before I trim them, and ask for cooperation if I dig a hole. And it seems that Mother Nature is quite willing to work with me when I treat her with respect in this manner.

EPILOGUE

Whew, what wisdom and insight on every page. It will take some time to digest all these treasured teachings. This book is one of those valuable reference guides to keep handy in your library for anytime you are in need of inspiration or direction. I challenge you to dust off your journal or locate that blank notebook and awaken to your god-self to realize your personal truths. It won't be long before you will have an abundance of profound writing, capable of publishing your own book!

I am so impressed with the quality of the participants in their willingness to access their inner being and send me their weekly answers. I'd like to express vast gratitude and huge thanks to all who participated and allowed us a glimpse of a very intimate part of their lives. I also would like to express my deepest honor to the source within. This presence in my life is more than I can express. I think upstairs has something to say here.

You all have participated in spreading my word, and a heartfelt thanks goes out to all of you. I realize that your participation was thanks enough, as it brought you and I together as one. I'm going to be a busy being, as many more will take part in what you all have presented in this book. Don't worry, I can handle it! My blessed people, your love for me propels my love for you. It is an infectious cycle that hopefully will spill over to all areas of your life and the people in your life. Love is grand, and if this book has assisted in this process that is all we can ask. Thank you, reader, for your interest and desire to do our work together. Get stuck? Just ask. I am only a keyboard or note pad away. My love for you will see you through your difficulties. Thank you again.

Thanks Upstairs.

Signed, Llovit

INDEX OF PARTICIPANTS

Babysteps/Huntsville/AL, 25

DJS/NB/Canada, 51, 52

Irishmossey, 31

Jack Aarron/USA, 29

Jay/Lismore/NSW/Australia, 18, 48, 53, 56

Jimmy L/Denver/CO/USA, 28

JofromAlaska, 44, 51, 60, 69, 90, 96, 106, 116, 153

Lennie/OH/USA, 21, 22, 49, 63, 71, 92, 95, 105, 114, 147

LittleSoul/Anadarko/OK, 32, 41, 49, 72, 91, 97, 107, 113, 128-139, 144, 155, 162

Llovit/WA/USA, 33, 36, 63, 66, 79, 125, 145

Marilyn/Amboy/WA, 40, 51, 57, 67, 88, 98, 103, 118, 156, 163, 166, 169

Norma/Mexico, 78, 142, 162

Patricia/NJ, 18, 66, 78, 108, 121, 139, 156

SAM/Clinton/Mass, 41, 54, 58, 73, 83, 99, 100, 109, 122, 143, 150, 160

Scott/Arizona, 39

Skeeter, 28

Tiaka/Japan, 47, 76, 89, 94, 107, 123, 153

www.ingramcontent.com/pod-product-compliance
Lightning Source LLC
LaVergne TN
LVHW011911080426
835508LV00007BA/478